CW01522520

'People will love this book.'

James Acaster

'Honest, hilarious and totally relatable. Simply wonderful, I related so hard to every chapter. I LOVED IT.'

Rosie Jones

'A really funny and honest book. A work of such importance.'

Jon Richardson

'An excellent book. I want to give it to everyone I know – from my teenage niece to my sixty-year-old dad. So brilliant.'

Maisie Adam

'A brave and vulnerable book by a very, very funny woman.'

Joe Lycett

'Suzi has managed to write a memoir that acts as confidante, agony aunt and your best friend in one warm, honest and beautifully written book.'

Jen Brister

'God, it made me laugh, and at the same time think, "Oh yep – that's like my little anxious brain box too," comfort and LOLs from one of the best in the biz.'

Ellie Taylor

Am I Having Fun Now?

Anxiety, Applause and
Life's Big Questions, Answered

Suzi Ruffell

Am I Having Fun Now?

Anxiety, Applause and Life's Big Questions, Answered

BLUEBIRD

First published 2025 by Bluebird
an imprint of Pan Macmillan
The Smithson, 6 Briset Street, London EC1M 5NR
EU representative: Macmillan Publishers Ireland Ltd, 1st Floor,
The Liffey Trust Centre, 117–126 Sheriff Street Upper,
Dublin 1, D01 YC43
Associated companies throughout the world
www.panmacmillan.com

ISBN 978-1-0350-3688-2

1 2 3 4 5 6 7 8 9

A CIP catalogue record for this book is available from the British Library.

Typeset by Palimpsest Book Production Ltd, Falkirk, Stirlingshire
Printed and bound by CPI Group (UK) Ltd, Croydon, CR0 4YY

Visit **www.panmacmillan.com/bluebird** to read more about all our books
and to buy them. You will also find features, author interviews and
news of any author events, and you can sign up for e-newsletters
so that you're always first to hear about our new releases.

For Mum and Dad

&

Alice and Peach, my two great loves.

Contents

Introduction

I was in a soft play centre with my daughter, who was three at the time. She catapulted from one side of the room to the other, barely stopping, occasionally squealing with delight. Breathlessly, she approached me, gestured to me to pick her up and asked, 'Mama, am I having fun now?' My first thought was: I hope *you* are, because we certainly aren't in a soft play centre on an industrial estate on the outskirts of Bromley, full of screaming, sweaty kids on the hottest day of the year, for *my* benefit.

I didn't have time to unpack all that so I just reassured her, 'Yes, darling, we are having a great time,' and whoosh she was off, up a ladder, down a slide and directly into a ball pit.

But her question stuck with me, long after dinner and long after bedtime, knocking around my head like a ping-pong ball. I felt pretty sure that she was having a good amount of fun every day, we prioritized it. I wasn't so sure about me. As Alice (that's my wife, you'll get to know her later) and I settled down for a night on the sofa, I asked, 'Am I fun?'

Alice looked at me, confused. I repeated: 'Am I fun?'

Alice paused *Call the Midwife*, knowing this conversation wouldn't be finished by the end of the opening credits. She breathed in and gently said, 'You're a great mum and a great wife but I think you might have more fun if you worried less. I think sometimes your anxiety stops your fun.'

She casually pressed play and was soon engrossed in Trixie and the girls on their home visits.

I didn't want my anxiety to stop the fun but I don't remember a time before it. I've known anxiety longer than I've known my wife, our child and all of my friends. I just assumed I would always be fighting it, one way or another. It wasn't usually a full-on punch-up, but more of an occasional jab in the ribs when no one was looking. A shadowy figure that only I could see, sneaking around insidiously, looking for the next thing to grab hold of. I *knew* it stopped me from 'living my best life', from 'seizing the day'.

Approaching forty, with a great marriage and child, I decided now was the time to really deal with it. I started regularly seeing a therapist and unpacking worries, hopefully to dispense with some and reorganize the others to make them more manageable.

This book was inspired by what I learnt about myself in those sessions. A collection of questions that I needed the answers to, questions I knew my friends had also wrestled with, questions I think you may have grappled with too. I knew that I wouldn't be able to uncover all of the answers alone so at the end of each chapter I speak to a real expert on the subject – psychologists, relationship experts, best-selling writers – to give me and you advice and tips on how to commit to life and have more fun while you're doing it.

CHAPTER 1

How do you know when you're worrying too much?

When I was seven, I killed my grandad.

I don't have many memories of him and even the ones I do have might have been made up in my head from stories my family told me. Jack was seventy-four when he died, which doesn't feel that old to me now but at the time he seemed ancient. He'd had throat cancer and had undergone a lengthy operation to remove his voice box, so he spoke with an electro larynx – a little machine you press into your neck that gives you a voice like a Dalek, C-3PO or a very, very, very boring man. The two main things I remember about him are that robotic voice, and his kindness. When I was six, he video-recorded the musical *Grease* off the telly for me because he thought I'd like it. He was right and it started a lifelong love of musical theatre. He'd taped it over one of his Western films on VHS which meant I didn't see the opening scene, with Sandy and Danny on that beach, until I was in my late teens. For me, *Grease* will always begin with a cowboy storming through saloon doors and a barman looking up in terror. It didn't make sense but it also didn't make sense that people clearly in their thirties were pretending to be high-schoolers. (Things are confusing when you're little. My cousin told me that Bowie, her white toy poodle, was actually her brother and I believed her for months.)

Gramps would let me sit on his lap while he was having a tea and give me custard creams on the sly without Mum seeing. Sometimes he took his teeth out and would do a hugely exaggerated gummy smile to make me laugh. It worked every time – I've always been a fan of slapstick. I'm told that in the midst of his treatment, while I assume he was feeling like utter shite, he went out of his way to go to the shops to get me some orange Lucozade. I had a stomach bug and it was the only thing I could keep down. (In my family in the early nineties Lucozade was considered medicinal.) Making an unnecessary trip to the shops for a radioactive-looking soft drink while enduring gruelling radiotherapy tells you everything you need to know about my gramps.

I wasn't actually with him the night he died: I was at a sleepover at Katie Burrows's house. Her parents owned some holiday apartments in a nice part of town and playing at hers was always a thrill. Katie would sometimes pinch the keys to one and we'd pretend to be grown-ups sharing a flat. It was the height of excitement for a seven-year-old. In the morning, Mum picked me up in her Suzuki Vitara. I loved that car, I felt extremely cool in it. Mum would put music on and we'd sing at the top of our lungs, throwing in hand gestures – I would even pretend to hold a mic. Our favourite was Diana Ross and the Supremes, which we played endlessly, until the tape snapped and the Suzuki vomited out the mangled cassette.

That particular morning, Mum's eyes were wet when she got out of the car. Katie's mum ran straight out and hugged her. Weird, I thought. I said goodbye to Katie and climbed into the back. There was no Diana Ross on the way home. In the kitchen Mum sat me down and explained that Gramps had died but that it was OK because he had gone to 'a better place'. More confusion for a little brain: there was somewhere Gramps considered better than here at home with us? The best place *I'd* ever been was Disneyland. We'd holidayed there when I was four, after Dad had had a particularly good year at work. I thought it was the greatest place in the world – I'd met Mickey and Minnie, Goofy, both Ducks and been slightly terrified by 300 animatronic dolls telling me how small the world is through the medium of song. We'd been allowed to eat sweets and ice cream to utter excess and go on ride after ride after ride. We'd bought hats emblazoned with our favourite characters – Mickey for me, Goofy for my brother, Joe. Dad got one with a fake ponytail coming out the back, which Joe and I found hilarious – truly, doubled-over, crying hilarious. Dad, always one to make the most of a gag, would toss the ponytail casually over his shoulder like he was Jon Bon Jovi. Mum found it toe-curlingly embarrassing which, of course, made us laugh even more.

I didn't think Gramps, whose favourite things were John Wayne films, darts and a pint of bitter, would like

Disneyland. And I couldn't think of anywhere else he'd prefer to be than home with us.

Mum told me that he would watch over me always, that he would always be with me. Which I found . . . troubling, frankly. My immediate worry was that there were other dead people watching over me too, maybe people I didn't know, maybe bad people. Maybe while I was in the bathroom. I imagined a ghost hanging out in the clouds above our house, looking down at me in our avocado green bath. From then on I was always sure to cover my bits with a flannel. I imagined a – what's the collective noun for a group of ghosts? a flock? a mischief? a horror? – a horror of ghosts all sat on my windowsill, watching me play in my room, maybe a couple of the more curious ones perching on the end of my bed as I slept, and I didn't like it one bit.

After Mum had explained how Gramps was living it up at ghost Disney, I noticed that our house was full of family. We lived in a lovely end of terrace in old Portsmouth, with red leather sofas and a heavily patterned blue carpet. Everyone was drinking tea, and Mum was offering sandwiches. Offering sandwiches is my mum's love language but no one was hungry and everyone was crying, especially Nan. She'd recently survived stomach cancer, but it had totally ravaged her body. She'd gone from a size 16 to an 8 when she had major surgery to remove three quarters of her stomach. She was so frail, her slight body moved with caution, like a little bird in a world that was far too loud and bustling for her. She sat at the kitchen table weeping into her teacup. I cuddled her. *'Gently, Suz!'* Mum shouted from across the room while slicing more tomatoes for more sandwiches that no one was going to eat.

Since Nan's op I'd been constantly told to '*be gentle*' around her. Apparently my hyperactive, distracted, clumsy demeanour isn't great for someone recovering from surgery and living with just a quarter of their stomach.

I couldn't bear seeing Nan, Mum and Aunty Jak so upset. I wanted to find a reason, I needed to understand *why* Gramps had died, to make sure it didn't ever happen to anyone else. The truth was that the radiation hadn't worked and the cancer had spread throughout his body. Tumours had grown in all his vital organs and eventually that caused them to fail, but seven-year-old Suz couldn't comprehend all that. So I decided it must have been *my* fault and the reason Gramps had died was because I had slept at Katie Burrows's house. If I'd just stayed home I would have saved him and probably even cured his cancer. Child logic.

It was the first thing I was truly anxious about. What I didn't realize then was that anxiety would go on to be my constant companion, into adulthood and beyond.

'*She's only happy when she has something to worry about.*'

My family have said this about me for as long as I can remember. I used to believe it. For a long time, it was justification for my excessive overthinking and tendency to catastrophize. If there wasn't anything obvious to worry about I would actively seek something out, like a detective on the hunt for angst. I was a Worrier. Worrying was what I did. It was the early nineties and my family didn't have the vocabulary for anxiety, or, for that matter, any other mental health issue. They certainly didn't have the tools to help me manage it, and that's not their fault. It just wasn't part of public conversation, at least not in Portsmouth. So, I was told *not to worry that I was a worrier* because that's just who I was. It's who most of my family are. We all worry. That's the vibe. Being told not to worry about worrying is a hell loop, worse than Crazy Frog on repeat in a submarine.

Gramps was the first person I knew who'd died, and it flipped a switch in my mind. All at once, the fragility of life became overwhelmingly apparent. I suddenly realized that people were dying all the time. Every day. Hundreds of thousands of people for hundreds of reasons. Old, young, rich, poor, every kind of person and there was absolutely nothing you could do about it. I was frightened that Mum would be next, that the grim reaper had hung around in Portsmouth waiting for the next victim – it was more than frightening, I was truly terrified. Before Gramps, I'd never even considered that my mum could die but once that macabre idea crept into my mind, it wouldn't leave. It argued squatters' rights. At school, in Year 3, my kindly teacher Miss Sampson would be reading from our class book, *Matilda*. I'd be laughing along at the thought of Mr Wormwood's hat superglued to his head, then the dark thought would slither in: *Mum might have had an accident walking back from school, mightn't she? That main road is always very busy. And Dad always says people are driving too fast so close to the primary school, someone might have hit her, she might be laying there in the street, blood coming out of her head, her eyes open.* I needed to do something. Sickness would wash over me. My skin would go clammy. I'd need to leave so I'd tell Miss Sampson I had a tummy ache. I'd burst into tears because my brain, or at least some of it, really believed the ghoulish story it had summoned. The school receptionist would ring home, and I'd wait at the front desk, sitting in a grown-up chair, feet not quite touching the floor, kicking my legs, counting how many kicks before Mum appeared and my heart could stop racing and this nausea would dissipate. Staring at the school gate, willing my mum to walk through it. Ten minutes later there she was. Smiling as she walked towards me. The relief would be so overwhelming, I would cry again. Mum would wrap me up in the safety of her arms and I could breathe a little calmer knowing that, for now, she was still alive.

When I wasn't at school, I vowed to never leave her side. It was the only way I could properly protect her. I started wetting the bed again, too, just what Mum needed when dealing with the grief of losing her dad: an unbelievably needy child and piss-soaked sheets. Often, I wouldn't even tell her I'd done it; just change my pyjamas, then sneak into Mum and Dad's bed and watch her sleep, the gentle rise and fall of her chest confirming: not dead, not dead, not dead.

Mum knew that I worried but I didn't tell her I had started making little deals with the world in order to keep everyone safe. If I managed to outrun the bus to the end of the street, Mum would live. If I managed to get all the way up the stairs using only the banisters, not once putting my feet on the carpet, Nan would never die. I felt it was my job to protect everyone. Which is quite a lot of pressure for someone who was still learning simple multiplication and occasionally spelling her name Zusi.

Little Zusi wasn't only worried about keeping people alive. I was also very concerned about the dead. We lived next door to a small church and I would often play in the church's front garden. One day, I noticed these great stones with names on them leaning against our house. Imagine my shock when I asked what they were and discovered there were dead bodies buried in the soil right next to our living room. I had seen the video to Michael Jackson's *Thriller* and I became very concerned that the dead were going to rise and potentially bust out a terrifying (if maddeningly catchy) choreographed number. Frightened, I asked Mum if zombies were under the ground just inches from our sofa. Mum reassured me that the graves were so old all that would be left was a skeleton. Ding, ding, new fear unlocked. I instantly became petrified of skeletons. Joe told me there was one inside me *all the time*, which, trust me, did not help.

One of the great things about having a big imagination is that I often create stories and ideas that I can genuinely see in my mind's eye, so specific and exact that they could be confused for memories. One of the bad things about having such a big imagination is that I often create stories and ideas that I can genuinely see in my mind's eye, so specific and exact that they could be confused for memories. At one point during primary school, I became convinced there was a ghost in my room every night. I imagined a hooded character hiding in the wardrobe then gliding over to me. I hated that it didn't have feet. I would often fall asleep with my eyes squeezed shut and the duvet over my head. Even now I am scared of the dark. When I'm on tour I have to stay in large busy hotels to feel safe. I don't mind being woken by the drunken cackle of a hen party getting back at 2 a.m., in fact I find it reassuring. I was once put up in a very old B & B after a show in Aberystwyth. It had clearly once been some sort of stately home, the architecture stunning but the decor suggesting we were visiting after its heyday. I don't think I need to tell you I found it creepy as fuck. I tried to get to sleep, tossing and turning while imagining Victorian ghost children at the foot of my bed. In the dead of night I was woken by a thud from the floor above me, but I was on the top floor. Above me was only an attic where there weren't any guest rooms. I heard a noise travel from one side of the ceiling to the other . . . Obviously it took me no time at all to work out that the aforementioned ghost children were rolling a ball to each other, just feet from my head. I promptly shot out of bed, jumped in my car and drove the 240 miles to my parents' house arriving knackered at 6.45 a.m. A few years ago, when we were buying our house, during the second viewing I asked the owner if anything weird or creepy had ever happened in there, much to my wife's embarrassment. I had to check. I'm happy to say, two years later no hauntings to report.

I can see now that my poor mum was dealing with a lot more than grief and a needy child. It was the early 1990s and interest rates had just sky-rocketed, which had a massive impact on the economy at large and on us at home. My dad has always worked with lorries and horses – for more than a century the Ruffell family trade was delivering coal with a horse and cart. Dad left school at fifteen to transport coal all over Portsmouth and the surrounding area. By then the family had upgraded to a small lorry. Often Dad would go to the posh end of town or just beyond it to 'the big houses', gorgeous Georgian piles, each with a flash car in the drive and a polished brass knocker. These were the customers who could buy coal in huge quantities, who'd never have to wait until payday or worry about running out. Most houses had a small bunker outside the front door but some of the big ones had a full-on coal shed in their back garden. Working with the black stuff all day, Dad would obviously be covered in soot. There were a handful of uptight, well-off women who wanted coal in their garden but didn't want a workman in the house, so he'd have to remove his coat and his shoes and they'd wince as this very young man struggled through their house with a hundredweight of coal, more concerned for their carpet than his well-being. They'd eye him with suspicion and hurry him out again, keen to not have 'his type' in their beautiful house. It must have been hugely shaming. But rather than getting jealous or annoyed Dad got inspired. *He* wanted to be the man with the flash car in the big house. He wanted that life. He didn't want to be the pitied boy in holey socks with a bag of coal slumped over his shoulder.

He was ambitious, and a workaholic, but also generous to a fault. Turns out it's hard to get rich when you're always the first to put your hand in your pocket down the pub. He wanted more. Always more. Over the next twenty years my dad slogged to build up his company, lorries mainly, and he owned a lorry park (literally a car park for lorries). Portsmouth is right on the coast so the perfect place for a lorry awaiting a load. When Dad had a little bit of money in his pocket, it was suggested he buy some land, maybe even a commercial property. The bank was lending and Dad, like Del Boy, really believed that this time next year he would be a millionaire. But that's not how it went. In the early 1990s interest rates climbed so high that Dad couldn't afford the repayments. The people who'd rented the commercial properties decided to downsize. The lorry park was half-empty. The lenders who'd happily bankrolled his ambition were now on the phone demanding their money back. Dad was swimming in so much debt he could hardly breathe. He had no choice but to declare bankruptcy and watch twenty years of grafting day and night slip down the drain. The nice car was gone, the lorry park, the lorries, everything except our house and I don't know how he managed to hold on to that. I do have a faded memory of bailiffs at the door. I imagine Dad's gift of the gab bought him a few more weeks.

This could have totally dimmed his ambition, it could have made him jealous and bitter but not him. My dad is very positive and while I imagine he was utterly gutted, he knew that if he could build up his wealth once he could do it again, so he set to work once more. He worked harder than ever before, driving all over the country, buying and selling lorries, surviving on five hours' sleep a night. I definitely get my keenness to succeed from him, I never feel more like him than when I'm hurtling down the M4 at 1 a.m. And I know that's when he feels most like me – he would always brag to his mates about the number of miles I had driven that week rather than the gigs I had smashed.

Retrospectively, I realize that he must have been totally at his wits' end: not knowing where the mortgage payment was coming from, how they were going to afford this week's grocery bill. He tells me now that there were weeks he barely slept. It must have been enormously stressful keeping everything afloat and not losing heart. But I was seven and yes, the interest rates were very high, Dad had lost his business and we had no money, but I didn't have time to worry about that. I was far too busy keeping everyone alive and hiding from ghosts. I was totally shielded from the financial fears indoors but I wonder now if I picked up on any of the stress my parents were working so hard to disguise.

I was fifteen by the time I risked going to a sleepover again. It had been eight years since that night at Katie's. I tried loads of times, even with family members, but I could never go through with it. It would get to 10 p.m. and the fear would crowbar its way into my mind. I'd be watching *Bring It On*, trying in vain to learn the Clovers' choreography, pretending to fancy the leading man, and attempting not to notice Eliza Dushku. I would be laughing, having fun, then I'd hear it, like the deathwatch beetle in Practical Magic, *tick tick*. Immediately overwhelmed, my brain would rustle up some horror. A house fire? A crash in Dad's lorry? A murderer hiding in the garden shed? I had no choice. I'd have to leave. My mum would be called. I'd pretend I had period pains. Once again I'd be waiting by the window, willing Mum to arrive. Back in the Suzuki next to her, I would feel like such a baby, so embarrassed and ashamed, but my main emotion was enormous relief.

So, anxiety has been with me for ever. It shape-shifts, morphing into different bogeymen reacting to different moments and experiences. Whether it was fear around my sexuality, or feeling like I'd never fit in, or my brain immediately jumping to the worst possible conclusion if someone doesn't answer the phone immediately, or having to push the front door and count to ten to convince myself that I have indeed locked it, or having to do 'my checks' before bed every single night, it's always there, lurking in the corners of my mind.

'My checks', by the way, is my pet name for my daily social media audit. It's a fear that somehow, unbeknownst to me, I have accidentally added a photo of myself nude to my

Instagram grid and everyone I have ever met has seen it, even though I am well aware I have never taken a naked photo in my life. Or that I have accidentally added a photo of my kid that I didn't mean to share with the world. Or that I have uploaded a picture of not only my bank balance but the long number on the front of my card and the three security digits on the signature strip.

Once I've checked my main grid and stories, and I am happily comforted that there isn't an unwanted image hovering around the internet, it's time for stage 2 of my checks (and I would say that even on a bad day this still feels a bit mad). At this point I'm compelled to check my activity log to make sure I haven't accidentally liked any comments or images that are aggressive or hateful. I would never have done this on purpose but because I worry, I have to check. Because what if I liked something that was prejudiced or violent towards a group of people who are already marginalized by society and someone thought that I shared those awful opinions and while I slept everyone else in the world heard about it and by the time I woke up everyone hated me. I dread opening my phone and seeing thousands of posts from strangers out for blood, my blood. I would try to explain but no one would believe me. People would stop coming to my shows. I'd lose all my work. Other comedians obviously wouldn't want to work with me because there would be this rumour that I was problematic, then the mortgage would be a struggle to pay and it would create a wedge between me and my wife, Alice. I would be sad but also angry. I would be unbearable. And after six months of my grey angry cloud over our house Alice would say my energy wasn't good for our daughter to be around, that my mental health was harming her, so I would have to move out and live in a bedsit with a ghost in a dodgy area where I didn't feel safe, which means I wouldn't sleep, making the anxiety even more prominent. My eczema would flare up and it would get really itchy and really sore as it rapidly spread across my arms and entire face, I wouldn't be able to stop myself from scratching it because the pain felt strangely satisfying. I would stop eating because that's what stress does to me, which would leave me gaunt and hallowed. And every time I saw my daughter she would wince and I would notice a fear in her eyes because Mama wasn't really Mama any more.

As I say, I am prone to catastrophize.

I'm a lot better now in some ways, but even these days, when I get home from a show late I always have to check on my daughter and wife to make sure they are safe. (I don't think listening to podcasts about serial killers and the paranormal has helped this. Why am I morbidly interested? Is it some sort of rush to stare directly into the belly of your greatest fear? It can't be sensible.)

I still live with low-level anxiety most days, it's the distant hum that scores my life. And sometimes it escalates; moments where I still feel like child Suzi, hanging off a banister, trying with all her might not to touch the floor. (Not that I'd attempt that these days, I don't have the upper body strength.) It flares up most when I am tired or feeling creatively unfulfilled. When my brain is knackered or if I have too much time, I do still revert to searching for something to worry about. But on those days I will lay on my back, legs on a chair and just breathe. It sounds so simple but it works. Then I will put on an absolute club banger, this week it was Becky Hill's 'Remember', and I will dance, dance really hard, by myself, in my bedroom, a dressing room or in my car (in a Highway Code safety-approved way) until I feel like me again.

. . .

I am going to chat to Dr Kirren Schnack, a highly qualified clinical psychologist and bestselling author. We meet on Zoom. I loved Kirren's book, *Ten Times Calmer*, and we kick off by me telling her how useful I have found it with my own anxiety. Kirren has a gentle manner that immediately puts me at ease.

I begin by asking her if it's normal to be very anxious?

'Oh, that's a great question,' she tells me. 'Because first of all, what's normal and who gets to decide that?'

To be fair, that is also a great question.

'I don't really think anyone is normal,' continues Dr Kirren. 'Everybody gets anxious because anxiety is a normal emotion. But what usually happens is that anxiety is triggered by a specific situation – so, let's say a job interview or an exam, or maybe having to socialize with lots of people. That event or circumstance would cause the anxiety, but it wouldn't be debilitating. You'd feel that anxiety and the nerves, but you'd do the thing anyway. And then once you've done it, your anxiety would just go back down to zero, or back to your resting level, what your norm is. And you wouldn't think about it every day.'

But how do we know what 'debilitating' feels like to different people? It took a long time for me to accept that I was perhaps *more* than just someone who worried a lot. Certainly, as a child, it would stop me doing the things I wanted to, like staying at my cousin's for a sleepover. And as an adult, often, the same sort of anguish still rolls around my head every day. I ask Dr Kirren when general anxiety becomes an anxiety disorder.

'There are specific criteria which have to be met for anxiety to be considered an anxiety disorder. The feeling has to be there for long enough that we could call it both "persistent" and "present". It might be three months or six months, but it's persistently there, the majority of the time. A "normal" experience of anxiety is where it's brief and it goes away. But if you have a disorder, you'd be anxious the majority of the time, and you'd develop specific behaviours in order to manage those feelings, like rituals: "If you don't do X then Y will happen."'

Ah. Like . . . running for a bus to keep your mother alive?

'Yes, or needing a lot of reassurance, like asking a partner, friend, neighbour or parent the same question over and over again.'

Huge shout out to my wife, Alice, here.

'[People with anxiety disorders] tend to ruminate and overthink a lot so their thoughts just go around and around, but they don't resolve the problem of whatever the thought is that's causing that problem. So you have this obsessive ruminating – we call it *thinking* where you don't lead yourself to a solution.'

This feels incredibly familiar.

I tell Dr Kirren that, often, the first indicator that my anxiety is building is not what's going on in my brain, but my body. 'Is that usual?' I ask her.

She tells me that we all have 'around five or six physical anxiety reactions' which are our particular body's default.

'For one person,' she reveals, 'those might be heart palpitations, dizziness, sweating, or needing to pee. For somebody else, it might be twitching and feeling sick. I'm sure you've heard of the fight-or-flight response. When you're anxious your body is getting ready for action: fighting back, or running away. Increasingly we are understanding "freeze" as a response too, especially following trauma. But for fight-or-flight your physiological system releases stress hormones, adrenaline and cortisol, which flood your body in order to physically bring about all the changes to prepare you for that action. We feel these as physical symptoms – such as muscle twitches, which people get because there is too much nerve energy. So, imagine you're sitting in a chair and you're really anxious because you had a terrible thought about somebody dying or because you don't know if you turned the cooker off. That kicks off your fight-or-flight response because you're telling your brain there's something to be scared of. Your brain gives you extra energy through the adrenaline and the cortisol, but you're not doing anything. You're still sat in the chair. But the nerve energy has to go somewhere, so your muscles start to twitch to expel that excess nerve energy.

'Sweating is an interesting one too, especially when we remember that our physiological responses have adapted and evolved over time. In a fight-or-flight situation, if your body is dripping in sweat and you're slippery, it's harder for a predator to hold on to you.'

This blows my mind. I had never considered that anxiety sweats are all about making it easier to slip away should I be captured by a wild animal . . .

'It's fascinating,' Dr Kirren agrees. 'Peeing, pooping and feeling sick are part of this evolutionary response, too. Your digestive enzymes switch off so that you don't feel hungry when you're anxious, because your body doesn't want to use precious resources on digesting food. It wants to use everything it has to fight off the situation.'

'But the thing is,' she continues, 'today, we don't really

need those fascinating things that happen in our bodies, so sometimes, some people have to teach our brains to switch them off when they're not needed. Otherwise, they persist, and become habitual responses to even the smallest of triggers.'

It's helpful to know that my anxiety isn't a freak occurrence but in fact, the product of thousands of years of evolution. Anxiety has been keeping my ancestors alive since the dawn of time but is there any benefit at all to me still suffering with it today?

'Definitely,' says Dr Kirren. 'We all need *some* anxiety. It helps you stay safe, put your seat belt on, check if you have everything you need or whether you've forgotten something important. It makes you double-check the time of your flight. Anxiety makes you think about the things you have to deal with and what you need to prepare. And that kind of anxiety is good. Exams and interviews are also great examples: if you're anxious, that anxiety can motivate you to prepare. We call this performance-enhancing anxiety.'

I wondered if my 'dancing it out' actually held any value and I was thrilled to see Dr Kirren say in her book, *Ten Times Calmer*, that 'Scientific studies show that dancing can be an effective way to reduce anxiety. When you dance your brain releases endorphins, which are natural chemicals that make you feel happy and positive. The physical movement of dance helps reduce the level of cortisol in your body, too, a hormone linked to stress and anxiety.'

Great news! Alexa, play some Kylie.

Whilst researching this chapter, I read up on what our

most common anxieties and fears are: poverty, criticism, ill-health, loss, old age and death all score highly. They *all* rang true for me, but the most specific one was death after Gramps passed away. I asked Dr Kirren how often death anxiety comes up for children.

'It's usually at around the age of eight or nine that a child figures out the concept of mortality,' she says. 'It's often set off by losing someone in their family. And there's a link between realizing that people die, and realizing that you yourself are going to die, that your parents will die. It's a very common fear – and one which underpins a lot of anxiety disorders. By that, I mean that if you go far enough down the worry trail – often worries about anything – you eventually reach the big one, our fear of dying.'

I'm well aware that I've done this. Much of my anxiety is around keeping people safe. It didn't make sense to try to outrun a bus to keep Mum alive, but that was the gut feeling.

We all know we're going to die one day, and so will the people we love, but, as Dr Kirren explains, our fear of death can hold us back from living any sort of life.

'You've got two choices,' she tells me. 'But to think about it all the time, to have our fear – whether that's of illness, failure, loss or anything else – sit in our laps, can be a kind of death of its own. Or we can choose to live a values-driven life, and do the things that matter most to us. And through that, death anxiety is reduced, because what you end up with is a *meaningful* existence.'

So the antidote to death anxiety is living, really living, the kind of life that you want, going for your dreams or to concerts or to the beach with your mates. Doing the thing that makes you happy.

I would love to write something poignant here but instead I am going to stop. My daughter is calling me, the sun is shining and she's desperate for a trip to the park and an ice cream. In the interests of living meaningfully, I am going to stop working and do just that. And maybe you should put the book down now and do something for yourself, or at the very least pop on your favourite band and have a boogie on your own.

Here are some suggestions:

'Rain On Me' Lady Gaga

'Everywhere' Fleetwood Mac

'Hold On' Wilson Philips

'I Am What I Am' Gloria Gaynor

'Feel the Love' Rudimental

'Cut to the Feeling' Carly Rae Jepsen

'You Forever' Self Esteem

'Holiday' Madonna

CHAPTER 2

Does peaking at high school ruin you for life?

(And did Kate Winslet make me gay?)

Peaking at school certainly wasn't something *I* had to worry about. As a teenager I had eczema, anxiety and dyslexia. Forget singing, dancing and acting; this was my triple threat. School was hell: I hated everything about it, other than the uniform. I loved my uniform. A pressed white shirt, tie in a Windsor knot, a blazer with an *inside pocket for pens*. There's an androgynous stylishness to a school uniform and I've always liked to look smart. For example, sitting here right now I am in a button-down shirt and pressed trousers because I have respect for my book and for you. I now realize I was an odd teenager, at odds with my place in the world, desperate to grow up, desperate to be away from the childish teenagers and their stupid social hierarchy while also desperate to fit in to it. I hated the bitches, the bullies and the teachers who ignored both. Like a lot of teenagers I was spotty, lanky and awkward, completely uncomfortable in my own skin. But what I really wanted to be was a chic French lady, on a bicycle, with a sausage dog and a bottle of wine in the basket.

While all the other girls spent their time deciding if they were team Britney or team Christina (heaven forbid you could like both), I wanted to be Marie (yes, I had named my fantasy French lady after the female kitten in *The Aristocats*) on her bike with her dachshund Claude (yes, I named him too). I'd seen the image on a birthday card in Clintons and decided that Marie had a perfect life, away from the prison of secondary school and the vulgar kids inside.

As I said, an odd teenager.

When I was twelve I auditioned for the local youth amateur dramatic society, Portsmouth Players. As soon as I heard there was a club that encouraged showing off I knew it would be right up my street. (Or *boulevard*, as Marie would say). I got in and began rehearsals for Wild West classic *Annie Get Your Gun*. I knew, immediately, that I had found my people, and they weren't like my fellow high-school pupils. They were theatrical, bombastic, funny, over the top, all the things that I tried to hide at school. And we all took it very seriously, which I loved. This wasn't a theatre club to mess about in, this was the real deal. If the real deal was rehearsing a show one evening a week for thirty weeks to perform it for two nights in the assembly hall at the local boys' school. I was one of the youngest in the group and I loved being surrounded by the bigger kids who were talking about GCSEs, getting drunk and propagating rumours of teenage pregnancy. What. A. Thrill!

The Portsmouth Players was the perfect outlet. I was finding school very hard. I am not sure it would have been noticeable to any of the other kids in my class but it was a daily struggle for my mum to get me to the front gate by eight-forty-five. I would cry, beg, plead for her not to take me there. I still wince when I remember one morning weeping openly as she forced me out of the car. As she drove off I could see her face in the rear-view mirror: she was crying too. No surprise then, that I used to bunk off quite regularly. They left the gates open: what did they expect? I would take off my tie (thereby immediately becoming totally incognito, right?) and wander around a supermarket. Being outside of school grounds and enveloped in the mundanity of everyday adult life would calm me. To this day if I am overwhelmed, a wander round the bedding section of John Lewis does wonders.

On one memorable occasion, I bumped into Mum and Nan in the big Tesco in Commercial Road. I particularly liked that Tesco because of how well-stocked the home aisle was. You could easily kill an hour sniffing candles, checking the quality of the towels and assessing the wide array of dishcloths and mops they had on offer. I turned into the condiments aisle to find Nan picking up a bottle of HP Fruity (lovely with an omelette btw). I tried to hide my face with an Old El Paso fajita kit but it didn't work. Nan gasped—

'Suz, you're meant to be in school.'

Mum turned round and was confronted with my body and an Old El Paso head.

'Suzi!'

The jig was up.

'For God's sake, Suz, not again!'

We stood for a moment: all three of us, not sure what to do. I offered an awkward, apologetic smile. Mum sighed.

'Oh well, it's gone twelve so you may just as well come and have lunch with us before you go back.'

A ham roll, half a packet of crisps and a cup of tea later and I was being walked back through the gates. No one even realized I had left. I had been gone upwards of three hours, but neither the teachers nor my fellow pupils had missed me. That was . . . telling.

My mum was never one for attendance discipline; she knew it was hell. She felt sorry for me. Other people, usually distant family members, would tell me school days were 'the best years of your life', that one day I would miss not having the stress and responsibility that comes with growing up. Even at twelve I thought: if that's the case, I may as well walk off the pier now. I vividly remember one Sunday evening in 1998 attempting to buoy myself up for the following day at school. Sitting in my room, on the end of my bed, I felt like I was running out of breath. I cried so hard I hyperventilated. I now know that was in fact my first panic attack. Hot tears, snot, the petrifying feeling of losing control. I couldn't put my finger on why I felt so overwhelmed all of the time: I just felt at odds with myself.

It was around this time that my nan gave me a worry doll. If you're an anxious babe like me you'll know what that is: a small doll about the size of your thumb. Before bed you tell your worry doll all of your worries then pop her under your pillow. In your dreams she is supposed to carry all your problems away. I sat on my bed, feeling silly but desperate to find a way to curb this constant anxiety. I told her about my fears around fitting in, my desperate need for approval, my constant concern that someone close to me was going to die, my worry that all of a sudden it was deeply uncool to like the Spice Girls and that all I wanted was to listen to 'Stop' on repeat on my CD Walkman, and the red hot fear about how much I liked Mel C, the fear that knew I wasn't like the 'normal' girls.

Let me tell you, that little lady was overworked. She was already exhausted and it was about to get a lot worse.

I went to see *Titanic* seven times at the pictures. That film is three hours fourteen minutes long. In January 1998, twelve-year old Suzi spent twenty-two hours thirty-eight minutes at the ABC Cinema Portsmouth watching a ship sink. To this day I can quote most of the film. I watch it every couple of years and it will always feature in my top five movies of all time, don't @ me. I cried hard every time. The first time I saw it I sobbed myself to sleep that night. I loved everything about the film, the love, the tragedy, Jack's class struggle, Rose's bravery, Jack and Rose putting two fingers up at expectation and deciding love was more important, that really camp scene where Rose's mum is doing up her corset, the boyish good looks of a young Leo.

But let me be honest with you. I was mainly there for Kate.

That winter sparked a crush that I still hold dear to this day, a crush I have walked through every moment of my life with, a crush I assume I will have until I die (an old lady warm in her bed). I love Kate Winslet, I am in awe of her talent, her intelligence, her elegance, her wit; and in my opinion, she is one of the most beautiful women on the planet. Now let me be careful: the last thing a full-time, card-carrying feminist would want to do is make a huge fuss about a woman's looks. It belittles her, it objectifies her, it makes me no better than a misogynistic man that thinks a woman's only worth is what is reflected back at her in the mirror but anyone with vision can see she is an absolute stunner! I have watched every film and series she's ever been in and read countless interviews with her, have watched acceptance speeches and chat-show interviews, every performance and appearance confirming that my crush will outlive us both. And it all started with her first line in *Titanic*, wearing that massive purple hat: 'I don't see what all the fuss is about. It doesn't look any bigger than the *Mauretania*.' That was it, boom, I was in love and I didn't even know what a Mauretania was. Now, I am not going to say that Kate Winslet topless made me gay – I wouldn't be that crass or disrespectful to one of the greatest actors of this generation – but that scene (THAT SCENE!) did have a profound effect on me. It's worth noting that the only boobs I had seen previous to that were my mother's and no offence to Ann Ruffell but it was a very different experience. I've since learnt that the Kate Winslet/Rose DeWitt Bukater passion isn't exclusive to me. I have spoken to countless lesbians of my generation who have confided that as teenagers they too felt a rush of blood to the head (and other places) while Jack sketched her like one of his French girls. I wonder if Kate Winslet knows the effect she has had on lesbians of the '90s and '00s? My wife is also a paid-up member of the Kate/Rose Society, in fact she once told me that if I left her for Kate, not only would she totally understand but I would have her full support. And that, my friends, is real love.

I must be clear, it wasn't just that scene. It wasn't only the nudity that knocked me sideways. It was the first time I had seen a woman own herself and her sexuality. In all the other grown-up movies I had seen, sex was something for boys to crave and girls to tease. Not Rose, she recognized her sexuality and she wanted to bang! Which I am sure you'll agree is super hot. I watched the film at the pictures again and again to check my feelings for Kate/Rose. The second time I watched it cried myself to sleep again. This time, though, it wasn't for the ship sinking into the Atlantic but for me.

It was the first time I was sure I was gay.

I feel I need to give you some context for this. Twenty-seven years doesn't sound like a long time ago but it was way before celebratory coming-out videos on YouTube, representation of queer families in any sort of media or many openly gay pop stars. In fact pop acts were actively pressured to stay in the closet. When I interviewed Darren Hayes, the brilliant lead singer of hugely successful '90s band Savage Garden, he told me losing his record contract was a direct result of coming out.

And being gay at school in the '90s was no picnic. It certainly wasn't a route to popularity. In 1998 Section 28 was still rolled out across every school in the UK. Section 28 was legislation that prohibited the 'promotion of homosexuality' or 'the acceptability of homosexuality as a pretended family relationship'. Basically, teachers weren't even allowed to mention that gay people existed and if, heaven forbid, any of those teachers were gay themselves, they had to lie, day in, day out, about who they were, because the government had decided with absolutely no evidence that they/we were a threat to children.

It's probably worth noting here that I went to a faith school, which I think added to the internalized homophobia I felt. The messaging in school was that the Catholic Church believed that same-sex relationships were a mortal sin and they would never bless a same-sex union because 'God can't bless sin'. The school was full of wooden carvings of white, ripped Jesuses on the cross. And whilst people weren't shouting Leviticus 18:22 – *Thou shalt not lie with mankind, as with womankind: it is abomination* – in the corridors, everyone knew that being gay was bad, unnatural and gross. Being called 'gay' was the worst and most common insult in the playground: maths was gay, the teachers were gay, Backstreet Boys were gay, taking your own lunch to school was gay, having school meals was gay (you were better off just not eating), boys with their left ear pierced were gay, taking Art GCSE was gay, trying at school was very very gay, as was Shakespeare, wearing a helmet while cycling and hats in general.

Everything was gay but nothing was actually gay, except for me and I was terrified.

It wasn't until I was in my thirties that I realized the effect this legislation had on me. I wasn't aware of it at the time but I knew being gay was too awful to even be discussed. Illegal whilst at school, in fact. It meant that for all of my teens, twenties and the early part of my thirties I carried a backpack of shame. Heavy, uncomfortable and sad.

By the time I was fourteen I was more aware of my feelings towards other girls. It was becoming more and more present in my every day. Kate, Alanis Morisette, Mel C and Jennifer Aniston had all become kind of screen savers for the brain. As soon as I was thinking of nothing in particular, I was thinking about them. I decided I had to fill my life with anything other than hot babes. I jumped both feet into performing.

This is how my week looked:

Monday
School, walk home listening to Alanis Morrisette, pretend I am in a music video on the bus. Do homework. Try not to think about girls.

Tuesday
School, then tap-dancing at Purbrook Academy of Dance, pick up Judy Blume's *Forever* and try to feel something, anything, about sex with boys.

Wednesday
School, then classical singing training, go home, stare at myself in the mirror while singing the entire score of *Chicago* with full choreography.

Thursday
School, then Portsmouth Players amateur dramatics society, deep joy, try to be cool. Remember money for the tuck shop.

Friday
School, then try not to think about girls – hopefully be invited to drink at the beach.

Saturday morning
Dancing – try to master the triple open-time step, hold in stomach throughout class so the teacher doesn't call me fat (I was a size 8).

Saturday afternoon
Nan's for cheese sandwiches and a packet of crisps, worry about how much Nan might hate me if she knew how much I was thinking about Kate/Alanis/Mel/Jennifer.

Saturday evening
Try not to think about girls (made harder by watching *Friends*).

Sunday
Have a roast dinner. Stare aimlessly at homework while listening to *Jagged Little Pill* followed by *The Very Best of Andrew Lloyd Webber*. Wash my hair, dread the start of the school week whilst watching *Heartbeat*. Try, and conclusively fail, not to think about girls.

It was a full schedule for a teen struggling with her identity. I managed to convince myself that I was only attracted to a handful of hugely successful women in the public eye, so rather than it being a lesbian thing I was probably just really inspired by them. Huge relief.

Lots of my school peers seemed already to be assured in who they were. The Goths were confident enough to be different, the sporty lads were so obsessed with football they barely registered they were at school, and the Year 10 popular girls were so plastered in make-up they looked old enough to buy booze and apply for uni. They walked around the school like they owned the place and let's be honest, they did. Retrospectively, I wonder if those girls were hiding themselves just as much as I was. They used Max Factor, I used a cloak of pretend confidence, always trying to make jokes before I was the butt of them, playing the clown so I had control of the laughs. The more I write and think about this period of my life the more I understand the root of my desire to become a comedian. What a bloody cliché.

I was a chameleon, constantly changing myself to fit in with whatever group I was trying to hang with that week. I made sure I was always busy, preferably so busy I didn't have any time whatsoever to think. That doesn't feel like something that's going to bite me in the arse in a future chapter, does it?

My hobbies outside of school were genuinely a saving grace. They gave me a purpose. I was making friends and it was great to feel I was making progress in dancing and theatre club. I looked forward all week to my Saturdays in a community centre on the outskirts of Portsmouth. I started to feel like one of the 'normal' girls.

But then I met Charlotte.

Charlotte was three years older than me and easily the best dancer at Purbrook Academy of Dance. She could also sing and act, and she was beautiful but, most importantly, she was kind and funny. I had a small (big) obsession with Charlotte. She was good friends with my cousin Sophie who also danced at the school, which meant I could go and sit with her/them whenever I wanted. Whether she/they wanted me there or not. Charlotte was hilarious and I was in awe. She would hold court, everyone in stitches while she did funny little act-outs of people we knew; she'd even have our formidable teacher in hysterics. I'd always suspected there was a currency in being funny and Charlotte proved it. Everyone loved her, just not quite like I did. I was crushing hard. Every time I saw her my pulse would rise, my cheeks would flush, the hairs on the back of my neck would stand to attention – and she had absolutely no idea. She saw me as her friend's quirky little cousin and I saw her as the love of my life. I would kill time after lessons in the hope of seeing her being dropped off in the car park: she'd jump out of the car and my heart would skip. Once, backstage at the Kings Theatre Portsmouth, she had a conversation with me whilst wearing only her underwear. I lost the ability to speak. I just smiled and nodded like the Churchill dog. Being near her thrilled me and horrified me in equal measure.

I loved my theatrical hobbies and spent my time at school wishing my life away. Because school is *hard*. Let's be honest, is there anything more c*nty than a group of teenage girls? There's usually a Queen Bee/Bitch who for some unknown reason, presumably because she has been ordained by Satan himself, calls the shots. She decides who is in, who is out and what is cool. And at St Edmund's she hated me. My mum would constantly tell me that the reason I found it hard to make friends was because everyone was jealous of my theatrical talents, a lovely lie to make us all feel better. As an adult I have quite a lot of sympathy for QB (Queen Bitch). She seemed that she was winning at high school, but her dad had just bought a Porsche he couldn't afford and left her mum for a woman less than ten years older than us. She may have been jealous, not of my 'theatrical talents' but because my home life was settled. She didn't know I was struggling daily with the reality of who I was. She did occasionally call me a dyke but as she also called me a slag, a slut and a whore, when I was still very much a virgin, I knew it was a lucky guess. Let's just say that evidence wasn't overly important to her slurs.

She was expelled from our school in Year 9. Briefly I felt enormous relief which quickly subsided when I learnt she was going to the rival, neighbouring school five minutes down the road, opposite my nan's block of flats, a school I had to walk past three afternoons a week. It had recently changed its end-of-day times because it was so common for a fight to break out on the railway bridge between the two. This meant I rarely saw her, but when I did she would shout abuse. One time she chased me with two other girls who, in the nicest possible way, looked rough as fuck, threatening to give me 'a proper beating' for thinking I was 'better than everyone else'. I outran them and hid in the bin cupboard in my nan's block. They were wrong about my self-esteem but underestimated my speedy little pins.

During Year 10 every girl at St Edmunds fancied Robbie Williams, David Beckham or Scott from 5ive. I was busy pretending to fancy Leonardo DiCaprio. I had pictures of him all over my bedroom but, being the cunning little teenage lez that I was, I had managed to keep Kate next to him in 90 per cent of the photos. Robbie, David and Scott were everywhere, on badges, on pencil cases; some of the more artistic girls had drawn one of them on the cover of their exercise books. Mine was covered with an offcut of Mum's wallpaper, featuring a black dog with sad eyes. Hormones were raging, and everyone was very into snogging, which I thought was gross. At under-eighteen parties teenagers would count how many different people they could 'get off' with. All around the room youths pressed up against each other, washing-machine tongues like feeding time at the zoo. Rank. A girl in my year got twenty-two snogs in one night; I couldn't stop thinking about the number of germs in her mouth. Every time I looked at her I imagined green bacteria doing somersaults on her tongue, the type you'd see in an advert for Listerine.

Worse than snogging, everyone was obsessed by sex: who is doing it, how they are doing it and where they are doing it. I found the whole thing both vulgar and terrifying. I hated being a teenager, I was spotty and felt disgusting, was constantly sweaty and my boobs were always sore (even though they were tiny, a fact I was constantly reminded of by Zach, a boy in my form group, who thought my tiny tits were not only hilarious but warranted discussion by the rest of the boys in my class – incredible he had the gall to do this while missing half a front tooth. Years later I would thank God for my little boobs while wearing nothing but tit tape under a suit.) I hated everything about school: the pupils, the lessons, the Catholic teachings, the buildings, the teachers, but mostly, who I was there.

There were two teachers with whom I became mildly obsessed because I suspected they were lesbians. One taught PE (shocked gasp) and one was in the science department. There was even a rumour they were a couple. They may have just been women with short hair and trousers boasting an unnecessary number of pockets but I was convinced. They were the first lesbians (assumed) I had ever seen in real life and I would try to bump into them, stalking the halls long after the bell had gone to get a glimpse of them. Then when I eventually did hunt them down, I'd find myself totally flummoxed, nod earnestly, then run away. I got the feeling some of the more religious teachers didn't approve of them. I have half a memory of one of them leaving. Playground chat suggested it was because they couldn't have lesbians teaching at the school. This may have been totally untrue but I believed it.

They were always kind to me. I didn't have a crush on them, though, I saved that for straight girls (this would be a recurring theme for the next decade). I just wanted to be near them, which made me feel seen but also ashamed.

Somehow within that shame there was a glimmer of hope, that I wasn't totally alone. I didn't feel like such a freak. I have tried and failed to find them both on social media over the years but no luck. So if you're reading this, thank you for being visible to me even if you were just straight ladies with gay hair and trousers from an army surplus store. Somehow it helped.

As I made my way up through the school, I found it harder than ever to make friends. I really felt as if no one liked me. I was constantly left out, never invited to parties, and I found not being part of a gang very painful. It was heartbreaking to me that I didn't have a best friend like everyone else. Retrospectively, I see that I was so busy hiding who I was, I didn't really let anyone get close. So I just flitted around on the edge of different friendship groups. Whilst it wasn't as pronounced as the Plastics in *Mean Girls*, there was a school hierarchy and I was nowhere near the top. To give you an idea, I occasionally had lunch in the drama room with the English teacher. I would always berate myself after, thinking it was the 'saddest thing ever' – using sad there as both the traditional sad to mean melancholy and the British noughties slang i.e. *your trainers are two-stripe, that's so sad*.

I was desperate to be invited to walk endlessly around the Cascades in Portsmouth on a wet Saturday afternoon. The Cascades was a glass shopping centre in Commercial Road, an oasis for any teenage girl: it boasted a Tammy Girl, a River Island, a food court, Woolworths and latterly a Topshop, the opening of which – I am not exaggerating when I say, was a genuine highlight of my teenage years. Finally, I could get trousers long enough to accommodate my lanky legs. I was wearing a lot of cropped T-shirts, low-rise jeans, boot-cut jeans (a look championed by Rachel Stevens – she has a lot to answer for) and a baker-boy hat. Sometimes I would team my look with a scarf the width of a tie and occasionally a belly chain. (For younger readers, a belly chain is a necklace for the gut: it's as bad as you imagine.) I dreamt of being invited for a SpudULike, a Slush Puppy and a browse around Athena. Athena was a poster shop – an indication of how committed my generation were to posters is that a shop dedicated to film, band and football posters didn't just survive but thrived until the financial crash of 2008. All the girls would stare wistfully at the same print, a black-and-white shot of a male model holding a baby. He was 'the dream' if your dream was a man with a muscly back holding a baby. Deep in denial and fear I would agree, 'He's well fit.' My awkwardness and vague attraction to several of the cool girls meant that my company was 'odd' at best and 'fucking weird' at worst.

For someone without a friendship group, lunchtime is a cruel mistress. Your choices are: walk the corridors pretending to look busy, or hide. Occasionally, though, when not lunching with Mr Griffiths or lurking in the loos praying nobody found me, I played football in the playground. At least for a while. One Friday (I remember it was a Friday because I proceeded to worry about it all weekend) I missed a shot and got called a 'stupid dyke'. After that I stopped having a kick-about at lunch. I knew being a 'dyke' was the worst possible thing to be, and had to immediately put a stop to any rumours. The insult spurred me into finding a boyfriend and getting involved in all the snogging I was so averse to. My first boyfriend was a very kind and caring boy called Dan. He had no idea he was a decoy but he made my school life much easier. He was quiet and confident and a real tough nut so if any of the boys were horrible about me, he'd offer to beat them up. Thanks, Dan.

Alongside kind but tough Dan, I was most grateful for theatre clubs and theatre kids who kept me sane. Mum knew I was finding school hard and she'd often organize fun stuff to do at the weekends in the hope that I wouldn't notice my lack of invites. One weekend we went up to London to see the matinee of *Grease*. Can you imagine anything more glamorous?! I don't remember much about the specifics of the show other than that they seemed to have cut the Western saloon scene opening but I know I loved it. Afterwards, we wandered around the back of the theatre in the hope of seeing the stars of the show leaving from the stage door. As we waited I noticed directly above the stage door was a street sign, but this one was different to any I had seen before. Above the name of the street it said 'Theatre Land'. I couldn't think of anything better than going to work every day in Theatre Land. The pink ladies fell through the door below, in fits of laughter and Juicy Couture tracksuits, the ones with 'Juicy' emblazoned across the arse in diamanté (pure class). They still had their show make-up on and their hair in silk scarfs, protected for the evening's performance. I couldn't get over the fact that they had just finished a show and were about to do it all over again. To me it seemed they had the greatest job in the world (it still does) and they were a team, they were friends. It was all I wanted. On the train home I read and reread the biographies of everyone in the show. I discovered almost all of them had been to drama school. So I decided that's what I needed to do. That week I called all of the drama schools I had heard of and requested prospectuses. I wouldn't be able to audition for another four years but I wanted a plan. Over those next four years I became obsessed with learning 'my craft' which is a very precocious thing for a teenager to say but I was determined/ desperate to get into drama school, leave Portsmouth and descend on the bright lights of London to make my fortune and find my tribe.

In my bid for escapism I watched a lot of American TV. *Ally McBeal* was a real favourite. Can you imagine my joy when the show's designated hottie, Nelle Porter, started experimenting with her sexuality? I would edge closer to the TV and have the sound barely audible just in case Mum overheard and popped her head in while Nelle was snogging Ling Woo, be still my beating heart. Although that was nothing compared to the thrill of learning that Portia de Rossi, the real-life hottie playing Nelle, was an actual real-life lesbian. Huge news! At that time I worked in a corner shop (yes, I wore a tabard) that sold every magazine you could imagine including *Caravan* magazine, *Coarse Fishing*, *Simply Knitting* and *Diva*, a lesbian monthly mag that I never had the confidence to open. I would, however, sit in the back room surrounded by caravan, fish and knitting literature and read trashy American magazines. I have a distinct memory of opening a copy to read a story about Portia's 'saucy lesbian affairs'. Fuck, yes! I thought, discreetly. Then I read an article about how coming out would affect her career, that studio bosses, film producers and directors would now view her differently, and that it would be questioned whether she could still play a leading lady (it's always a given that leading ladies are straight). Portia had become a punchline in late-night shows, the same way her wife Ellen had years earlier. Two women I highly admired were ridiculed for being out, for having the audacity to be themselves. It seemed obvious to me that being an actress and a lesbian were mutually exclusive. I decided then and there, sitting on a box of Walkers Original, that it was impossible for me to be both an actress and a lesbian. So I chose to swallow my feelings for Kate, Charlotte and any other girl I had noticed. I would become a hugely successful actress. So convincing, in fact, even *I* would believe I was straight.

But I do often wonder about those girls who breezed through school, who were popular, who seemed untroubled, and whether they were having their own personal nightmare too. Was the weight of being the QB actually a lot for a teenager to bear? Those teens who were dealt an easy card at school, the ones who had friends and no big, crushing secret. The ones who weren't afraid of who they were. I wonder if not peaking at school is actually helpful for the real world. A lot of my friends are professional stand-up comedians, or actors or writers. Lots of them have faced adversity. They've been outsiders in one way or another, and I think that's fuelled, in part, their success. Does feeling separate give you a sideways view of the world that helps generate creativity? Maybe those lonely long lunchtime walks were actually my greatest gift, that the feeling of being 'other' gave me ambition and determination to find my strength. And I don't believe it's only people who end up showing off for a living that can turn their outsider-ism into a superpower.

. . .

I spoke to Natasha Devon, campaigner, radio presenter and author of books like *A Beginner's Guide to Being Mental* and *Yes You Can: Ace School Without Losing Your Mind* to find out more. Natasha has spent years travelling around the country speaking to young people and witnessing their interactions. I wanted to know if she thought peaking at school might leave you less prepared for adult life.

'I think what school does is silo us into very specific types of people, almost genres: very specific tribes and if you are outside of that, it's an incredibly isolating experience. But I also think that if you are *within* the prescribed and accepted stereotypes, it can still negatively impact you, because it doesn't allow you to grow and flourish outside of that. So yes, I do think that people who have their best experience at school are maybe not living their best lives.'

Jackpot! Suck it, girls who didn't invite me to their Pizza Hut birthday!

I am kidding but I have always wondered whether feeling that isolation in my school years made me more resilient as an adult.

'It taught you to think for yourself,' suggests Natasha. 'The teenagers that I meet who tell me their friends are the most important thing in the world to them also tend to be the ones who say, well, my friend said this, and therefore it must be correct. Even if what they are doing is damaging or morally wrong. The code of ethics or the code of conduct within that friendship group is more important than anything else. And when they hit university or work or whatever's waiting for them next, and suddenly that tribal code disappears, they may have less of an ability to think critically for themselves.'

Of course, for me, as well as the usual teenage stuff of trying to infiltrate friendship groups and stay on top of school work, I was struggling with my sexuality. Natasha also identifies as queer and I asked her how that plays out in the classroom.

'It's adolescence. It's when you get horny, essentially, and it's always so mad to me that that's also when you start studying for your GCSEs. It's like, so . . . I've got this big dopamine spike. I want to hump the fridge. How am I supposed to concentrate on my revision? I knew before I was a teenager that I'd had crushes on women, but it was around that time that I was like, oh no, this is a definite *sexual* attraction, and that's what I hear from most other queer people I talk to, too.'

Teenagers are juggling so many emotions all the time. I remember feeling exhausted at school and now I think I can understand why. School was an incubator for my anxiety – even now, as I'm approaching my forties, feelings of inadequacy snap me right back to that green uniform and bad skin. But it seems bizarre that being 'left out' more than twenty years ago still affects me in some way.

'It's because you laid down a blueprint back then that your brain still defers to,' says Natasha. 'You were discovering who you were and trying on different identities. The reason that we've evolved to have difficult or unpleasant emotions is to teach us something. That's why we feel stress, guilt, shame. All those icky emotions are your brain saying: don't do that again.'

She tells me there are two reasons our brain hangs on to these feelings for so long.

'Firstly, there's the neurological aspect: it's an incredibly important time in our adolescent development. For people who are developing along ordinary pathways, your body produces this huge dopamine strike, which brings about impulsivity, at around fourteen years of age. And there's a reason for that. What nature wants is for teenagers to take high-risk decisions with poor judgement. Because it's by making those mistakes and having the kind of courage to take on risky experiences that they establish independence from their families and discover who they are.'

So, because how you feel at that age is so important for moving you from a child to an adult, the brain holds on to it?

'Exactly. And it's a chemical thing too. This is really icky, but it's partly to stop you from having sex with your parents, making you find you them really annoying. You often hear teenagers saying: "My friends are the most important thing to me in the world," and they're not making that up. That's chemical: nature wants them to establish their own tribe, outside of their immediate family.'

But what did that mean for me, someone who felt they didn't *have* a tribe? I ask Natasha if she thinks that's why I focused so completely on a life beyond school, and on my hobbies.

'I know how obsessed you get with your passions and again, yes, it's a tribal thing. You want to be able to say: "These are my people. I belong." I remember when David Bowie died and there were loads of Bowie tribute concerts. I went to one, and when I looked around the room I thought: there's nothing that unites all of these people apart from the fact I can tell that they were all people who didn't fit in at school.'

It turns out that what I was actually doing when while lacing up my tap shoes and learning the alto line for *Me and My Girl*, was searching out my tribe. And it actually makes perfect sense that these are often the emotions I come back to, time and again.

'It's because you were going through so much neurologically and chemically,' Natasha reminds me. 'Those experiences that you have in your peer groups during that time do imprint on you in a really major way and it's so intense because it's the first time you've ever felt those feelings.'

I wish I could call my teenage self on her silver Nokia 3210 and let her know that this intensity is normal and that school isn't for ever, that experiencing discomfort, boredom and all those other horrible feelings is just part and parcel of life.

I would tell her that this resilience she's building, while endlessly wandering around the school on her own, creating little worlds in her head, trying to make people laugh to keep the anxiety at bay will, one day, come in really handy.

I would also tell her the Kate thing stays for life and, incredibly, that woman just gets better with age.

CHAPTER 3

Does living a lie actually make you sick?

Chichester College had a brilliant drama department and the highest rates in the area for getting students into top drama schools. I'd left school, and just had another two years to get through before I could head to London and start my journey to Theatre Land. College was fun – all I studied was Drama and Contemporary Dance (both really useful in the real world, actually), and for the first time ever I was top of the class. I found the work enjoyable. Getting A's was easy, which was lucky because I was very, very distracted. I had met a girl.

I could tell Amy was 'like me' before we'd even said hello; something to do with how she moved or talked or dressed. We looked each other in the eyes for slightly too long and both instantly saw an understanding, a vulnerability, an affinity that we knew we had to keep secret. Our first kiss was in her bedroom. The walls were yellow and covered with posters of Blink-182 and Sum 41. Above her bed was a huge poster of P!nk in a crop top staring down at us as we squeezed onto a single bed. We lay chatting, so close we could feel the warmth of each other's breath on our faces. We lay there for hours, both desperate but too nervous to make the first move, to out ourselves. Eventually Amy found the courage; she leant in and pressed her lips on mine. My heart was beating so loudly it rang in my ears, and I worried that her parents in the downstairs living room could hear it. My body came alive in a way that it never had before, like every nerve had received a pulse of electricity. Her soft hands on the small of my back made me light-headed. That kiss confirmed everything I'd questioned in myself. Kissing Amy felt so natural, so right, and being next to her gave me a comfort that had been a stranger until now but we *had* to remain a secret – people couldn't know the truth. What would they think? What would they say? I didn't want to find out. Our covert relationship lasted for nearly a year. There were moments of complete elation, of excitement, of all-encompassing pleasure, and other times when I was utterly repulsed by what we were together.

I ended it the day my dream came true. I got accepted into drama school, I was moving to London, I was going to be an actor, I was going to find my people and no one and nothing could stop me. And there was absolutely no way I was going to arrive as a lesbian. I couldn't be *that*. I cruelly told Amy it was a phase. That I wasn't really like *her*. That I was just trying it, that regardless of what I had whispered next to her in bed at night, I didn't have feelings for her and I didn't want to do *it* any more. I begged her not to tell anyone. I cried a lot that night. I was so happy and so sad.

It wasn't enough to just not be a lesbian, I felt I had to actively prove to everyone and most importantly myself that I was straight. Simon worked in the coffee shop next to college. He had a kind smile, ocean-blue eyes and a charming Irish accent. Flirting felt easy with him. He'd give me coffee on the house and make me laugh. I would find excuses to go and see him between classes. Making coffee in Chichester wasn't his plan, he too had been seduced by the bright lights of London. He'd recently qualified as a solicitor and was moving there in the summer to begin his career. It felt like a sign, these two young ambitious people heading to the capital to pursue their dreams – we should do it together.

Eight months later, I was packing my bags for London. Simon had moved in with friends in Clapham a few months earlier, and I was moving to Streatham – just round the corner, more or less – with people I met on my course induction day. I drove my Nissan Micra full of all of my worldly possessions, the CD player blasting out the Original Cast Recording of *A Chorus Line* the whole way. Mum cried as I left, but nothing could bring me down. I was doing it. I was jumping with both feet into my new life. Driving up the A3, everything felt so exciting, so possible, my life was about to begin. All I had to do was ignore what had just happened with Amy and my lifelong commitment to Kate Winslet. Ignore the fact that intimacy with Simon felt foreign, that sex felt like it wasn't really happening to me, like I was a bystander in my own bedroom, that it seemed to hurt not just my body but my very being too. Ignore what I longed for, noticed, desired. That was all. Easy.

Simon was a kind, smart, funny, charming guy who I loved and I was determined to believe I could be with, properly. And for a while it worked. During the first couple of years at drama school I was so preoccupied with learning as much as I could, impressing the teachers and making friends who actually liked me, that I really believed I had got the upper hand on my sexuality. I loved his company. In the second year of training we moved in together, we travelled together, we laughed, we made plans for our future. I often thought what a great dad he would be. Mum and Dad liked him. This is enough, I told myself, this is definitely enough.

But then I met Bec.

Bec managed the bar I worked in every weekend and she was the thing I feared the most – an out, happy lesbian. Initially, I hated her. She frightened me. I thought she was coarse and arrogant but she wasn't, really. I just couldn't stand being around her.

Some of the worst homophobia I have experienced has been from people I suspect are struggling with homosexual feelings, and for a while, I was one of them. I loathed seeing happy queer people and would occasionally mock lesbian stereotypes to my friends. I never feel surprised when an openly homophobic politician is caught with his pants down in the company of a gentleman caller. It's not a hard and fast rule but some straight people's obsession with the LGBTQIA+ community feels pretty gay to me.

So much homophobia – and I include the way I sometimes felt in my early twenties in this – is driven by fear. Look at sections of the right wing, both here and abroad, who are obsessed with the 'traditional family' and its values. The worst thing they can imagine, the thing they're most scared of, is having a queer child. Their greatest fear is my parents' reality. They think that children even seeing someone like me – today an out, happy gay person – might make *them* gay too. I might give them ideas. Boys might want to wear pink and dress like Elsa, and the girls might wear collared, checked shirts and – heaven forbid – cut their hair.

That's not how it works.

I didn't know any lesbians when I saw Kate in *Titanic*. I didn't really know it was a thing for women. I knew about gay men: I knew they were funny, I knew it was allowed, hey, even encouraged, to have a gay best friend (as long as it was a boy) but I also knew they were called poofs and fags, and mocked behind closed doors. In short, *I* was the first lesbian I knew and I had never been given a blueprint or an instructional manual (which to be fair, the DIY lez part of me would have really appreciated). I had a very traditional family. Dad worked, Mum stayed home to raise us, 2.4 children, one girl, one boy. My mum is very girly, my dad is a blokey bloke. Perhaps unintentionally the gender norms in my house were very pronounced. And that's without considering the wider world, that every TV show, song, film, book, even every game my brother and I played on the Super Nintendo, every family I knew, everything I consumed as a child and young adult, pushed the straight agenda, pushed the idea that being straight and having a heteronormative life wasn't just expected, it was demanded. And lo and behold, despite the constant emphatic messaging that straight was really the only way I still turned out gay. I was, however, at this point in my life, absolutely bloody terrified.

'You're gay, right?' Bec asked during our first shift together. She could see it in me. Her gaydar pinged. Like that moment that Amy and I locked eyes across a classroom. An understanding, an affinity.

My palms started sweating. I felt sick, I went weak all over. I felt a lot like Eminem in 'Lose Yourself'. My dry mouth just about managed to croak out: 'No, I have a boyfriend, we're gonna get married one day'.

She shrugged.

'OK.'

I went home and demanded sex, attempting to shag myself straight. It was about four weekends later that I kissed Bec in the pub cellar while struggling to change a barrel. It was electric. Unbelievably sexy and horrifying. Like *American Horror Story*. We then had a snog every shift. Pull a few pints, clear some tables, deliver chicken wings to a group of drunk mates, engage in hot passionate lesbian smooching next to various kegs, then swim in a sea of deep shame until the next week, when we'd start the merry dance again. These were my Fridays and Saturdays throughout autumn 2008. Every time I kissed Bec, Simon got laid: part guilt, part shame, part apology, always missionary. It was so confusing. I'd cry in the shower after the sex, then get into bed for a cuddle.

Simon was such a kind soul, and we really did have a connection. Alongside everything happening with Bec, and going on in my head, I still wanted to be near him. And it wasn't only about trying to be straight. I was also away from home for the first time. He'd taken the place of my very close-knit family when we moved to London. He represented home to me, and despite my desire for women, I craved the safety of his arms. You might judge me or dislike me for leading him on and I understand that. For a long time I felt enormous guilt for the double life I led back then. The fling went on for months. But I just couldn't cope with who I was. So much longing and self-loathing. My brain was all over the shop. I started smoking which looks cool but isn't and I was drinking a lot. I lost weight and the eczema on my face was furious about the fags and booze. I would also occasionally vomit, just chuck up my guts. The enormity of coming out, of telling everyone my secret, would occur to me, and my body would simply expel everything I had eaten that day. It was physically saying: 'don't do it!'

I was also reading a lot of Sarah Waters. There was so little lesbian representation in the media, that the people I felt most connection to were fictional characters from the Victorian era. Katy Perry's 'I Kissed a Girl' was at the top of the charts and this heralded a new kind of awful: straight girls kissing at house parties for the sexual gratification of boys. I am sure Katy Perry is a perfectly nice person. I like her music and I have watched her tour documentary twice but that song, that fucking song, it haunted me. Everywhere I went it blasted out, emboldening my internalized homophobia. Telling me by simply existing I wasn't a good girl. But I *was*. Other than secretly cheating on my boyfriend, that is. I was working hard at drama school, not doing drugs, checking both mirrors before changing lanes. I didn't want to hear it.

Despite the fact that I was having weekly snog session with Bec, I didn't want to think about kissing girls, ever. I certainly didn't want to see my female friends getting off with each other and God forbid, I didn't want to kiss any of them myself. What if they could tell? What if we kissed and I looked too into it? I finally had friends, best friends even, and I didn't want to lose them because of something I couldn't control. So I took that well-trodden route and said I didn't want to kiss girls at parties like the other straight girls in my friendship group, because it was gross and gay. Stay classy, Ruffell! Selma Blair and Sarah Michelle Gellar in *Cruel Intentions* didn't help. For younger readers, *Cruel Intentions* is a great late-'90s movie about rich kids, school bullies, homophobia, racism, love and a very odd sexual dynamic between step-siblings based on a novel from the 1780s. Obviously, it was an instant hit. Selma and Sarah had a long, wet snog which only encouraged the theory that everyone should be kissing and that boys loved to watch.

It's strange when you realize your sexuality is a kink to someone who has nothing to do with it. 'Lesbian' is frequently one of the most searched-for words on porn sites across the world. I knew that men found lesbians hot way before I eventually came out. And I worried that people would think I was coming out for attention, attention from men (which in my opinion is the very worst kind of attention).

A case in point: years later, having come to terms a bit more with my identity, I was in a bar, on a date with a woman. A huge man, in my memory he was at least seven foot but probably in reality closer to six, had been watching us since we arrived. I noticed him walking towards us in my peripheral vision. He greeted my date and me like we were old friends and offered to buy us a drink. We declined, carefully, in that way that women have learnt is safest to say no to men without belittling them or hurting their feelings. But he wouldn't take no for an answer. He positioned himself directly between our bar stools and casually draped his arms around our backs, his hand resting on the side of my ribs, close, intimate, intimidating. He spoke conspiratorially, with the intensity and unfounded confidence of someone who'd had at least three lines of Colombian marching powder. 'Come on, girls, have a drink with me? We could have some fun tonight.'

We exchanged a weary look.

'What's wrong? Have you got boyfriends?'

I laughed. He was clearly *very* drunk – I had an undercut and was wearing Doc Martens.

'Wait, are you together?' Clang! The penny dropped. We nodded awkwardly. We weren't really 'together', it was our third date, but now wasn't a time for semantics.

'Lesbians! Brilliant.' I have no idea why he thought this was brilliant. We were both exclusively attracted to women! We weren't going to get off with him!

Maybe he was an ally, I hoped, someone so committed to improving the world for LGBTQIA+ people that when he heard someone come out he couldn't help but publicly rejoice.

'I think we three should go home together and have some fun.'

Maybe not.

In that moment I wanted to tell him to fuck off, that my existence isn't a kink or a fad and it certainly isn't something for his sexual gratification. I wanted to tell him that interrupting two people on a date and suggesting a threesome is not only unbelievably rude, it's disgusting, offensive and homophobic, that I truly doubt he would even consider doing that to a straight couple on a date. Of course he wouldn't, presumably because he has respect for men. I wanted him to know that the idea of having sex with him not only gives me the ick but it makes my blood run cold and that the feeling of his massive hands, his rough fingers rubbing the small of my back, inching round to my bare ribcage, makes me shudder, makes me want to throw up, join a convent and take a vow of celibacy. But of course I said none of that. As two women out on our own we knew we had to play nice for fear of ridicule, slurs or, in the worst cases, violence.

We simply smiled and offered a polite no, thanks.

He responded sloppily: 'I love lesbians, come on, it's my birthday.'

Hilariously, he thought that might tip the scales in his favour. Now, I love birthdays but it was still a no from us. He pleaded – at one point he offered to beg. It was baffling that he thought he could talk us around. He got more and more aggressive in his advances, like we owed him something. He seemed to think it was his right to shout into our faces that he worked with a gay guy who was actually really nice and they were mates, so he couldn't possibly be homophobic. 'I am never too friendly though, I don't want to give him the wrong idea,' he laughed.

I try not to judge a book by its cover (although if that's the reason you've bought this one – cheers, babe!) but he was pig ugly. He looked like a witch had turned a bullfrog into a human man. I doubt very much that the 'lovely gay at work' considered them to be friends and I can assure you that, whoever he was, he had no interest at all in this man's coke-shrivelled mushroom cock and his appalling personality.

I could tell that the only lesbians he had spent time with previously were ones that live in the screen of his laptop, the ones who are delighted for a man to jizz on their tits. I hope this doesn't come as a shock to too many of you but those women aren't lesbians. He went on to say that he'd always wanted to 'watch lesbians in real life' like we were rare flamingos at London Zoo. He bothered us relentlessly for the next thirty minutes, until *we* had to leave.

I digress. Back to twenty-year-old me, stressing and vomming in Tooting.

Drama school was situated in an old Gothic castle. It was rumoured to be haunted which only added to the thrill. I was in a movement class in the great hall, laying on my back, limbering up, when it hit me like a bolt.

I could not go on like this. I couldn't bear the weight any longer. For the last few months I'd felt different, as low as I'd ever been. I thought I was putting on a pretty good show, pretending everything was fine, but friends kept asking if I was OK and I had made a point of not going back to Portsmouth at the weekends because I knew Mum would know something was up. I was very aware that drama school was my dream and I had put a lot of pressure on myself to appreciate the experience and to enjoy every minute. Unlike my school days, these really did have the capacity to be the best of my life. But I felt hollow, totally disconnected. At that moment, lying on a dusty floor, I realized I had to do something about it. I had to deal with these feelings.

I wonder if you are reading this thinking: Suz, it's really not that big of a deal, you're gay, so what? But it's huge, it's especially huge if you don't know anyone else like you. It's very lonely. As soon as you say it out loud you become 'other', you know that some people will hate you before they even meet you, that laws have been written to keep you away from the general population (more on this later), that some people believe even knowing you exist is damaging to children.

If you're reading this and you're straight, I'd implore you to stop and take a moment to imagine how that feels. No wonder I was scared.

I have friends who have lost family, friends or employment because they came out. You only have to look at legislation across the globe to see that people lose their lives, too, because they have been brave enough to admit who they are.

The first person I tried to tell was a drama school friend. We were in my Micra, heading to the McDonald's drive-through. The driver's side door had been broken for some time so I had to get in and out via the passenger door. If five of us were travelling together, when we exited it looked like clowns getting out of a circus car. On this occasion it was just the two of us. I hadn't planned to make an announcement but the desire to come out had been buzzing around my head, getting louder and louder by the day. I had held this secret in my gut for so long that I had to get it out. Increasingly, I knew it was only a matter of time before it crawled up my throat, prised my mouth open, and spewed out.

We drove past a billboard for the movie *Mr and Mrs Smith* – Brad Pitt and Angelina Jolie, both so hot, looked down on to the road, smouldering.

'She's so fit,' my friend sighed. This was my moment, an opportunity. I could casually, *very casually*, mention that I liked women as well as men. (I had decided that adding that I liked women too for a while would be an easier way for me to slowly edge out of the closet. I now realize this is problematic for bisexual people and often their identity is used as a stepping stone for someone like me but then, in my twenty-year-old brain, it felt like the safest option.) I agreed, 'So fit.'

OK, Suz, I thought, no time like the present, dip your toes in that gay water.

'I'd go gay for her,' I said, pretending not to be nervous.

'Oh, me too!' she agreed. I had told someone, in a round-about way, sure, but I'd said that I fancy a woman out loud. I breathed deeply, I think my shoulders came down several inches, maybe even a foot. Deep relief! Until my friend added: 'But I wouldn't go down on her, no proper lesbian stuff, that's nasty.'

As quickly as my shoulders relaxed they shot back up. My breath shallowed and I jumped back in the closet and bolted the door.

'Oh yeah, totally, it's nasty,' I agreed.

The first person I actually told was Amanda. She was one of the older people in our year and, being one of the youngest, I gravitated towards her because it felt like she had a grasp of the world. I was at her flat in Earlsfield, South London. She was making bangers and mash for tea – she'd often invite me round to make sure I was occasionally getting a proper dinner.

With no provocation, standing in her kitchen . . . I burst into tears. My deepest secret suddenly came tumbling out. I was gay, I had known it for ever and I was scared. I was worried all my new friends wouldn't like me, that my mum and dad would stop loving me, and what would my nan think? That I'd hurt Simon, and lose him as a friend. That I didn't really know any lesbians, other than potentially two of my old teachers who might just have had short haircuts and many-pocketed trousers. That I was frightened this would change my life, that I was frightened I would be lonely. As I voiced that last thought I realized that, under-neath it all, that's what I was really afraid of: that I would have a sad and lonely life, like my aforementioned Victorian lesbian friends from literature. Amanda just held me and let me cry. I explained how trapped I felt and that I didn't know what to do. I had moved in together with Simon six months earlier, in a desperate bid for a straight life. Amanda cuddled me, reassured me and listened to me. She was a true friend, and her acceptance helped change everything. I had told someone the worst and the world had continued to spin. I cried some more. We ate our bangers and mash.

Breaking up with Simon was awful, but, after I'd finally come clean to Amanda, I knew it was time. I didn't give him the reason. At the time I told myself I didn't want to add insult to injury but now I wonder if I was scared of his response. He'd never said anything to suggest he was homophobic, but I couldn't bear the idea that he might be. I moved out of our flat and turned up on a friend's doorstep, so sad, but also so relieved. Bec and I dated for a couple of months. She introduced me to loads of her gay and lesbian friends and to London's brilliant queer nightlife, Candy Bar, Heaven. I have such a clear memory of going to G-A-Y when it was still a night in the Astoria. Girls Aloud were playing so it was utterly rammed. We went to the upstairs bar to get a drink and I looked out across this sea of people, a sea of people that were like me, thousands of them, dancing, laughing, being free. Despite 'Sound of the Underground', the cacophony of cheers and screams of delight, the sheer number of non-stop flashing lights, the occasional nudge of someone a little merry making their way to the bar, I felt peace, the kind of Zen you usually only encounter at a Mediterranean yoga retreat.

Bec and I broke up when she returned to her home in Cape Town. Although our relationship was brief I will always be grateful to her for showing me that there was a way to be myself fully and that happy gay women existed. Loads of them.

Today, I am very aware I speak from a place of privilege. I live in a country where we have same-sex marriage, where queer people can become parents, where most of the population is largely tolerant, although I hate the idea that people like me should be merely 'tolerated'. But even in this largely accepting society, being your authentic self and coming out is stressful. I don't think that's only down to the risk of being rejected by the people you love. I think it's also because it reduces the queer experience down to sex. And that's just awkward.

Anyone in a loving relationship reading this – straight, gay, somewhere in between – knows that sex isn't the only dimension of your love. That first year after a baby, it can be a dimension you totally forgot existed, a dimension that feels like it's from, well, another dimension. Shout out to the tired parents reading this. (Go to bed, this book will still be here tomorrow.) But when you first start telling people, sex is often the first thing they consider.

Even if you're lucky enough to have the most understanding and open-minded parents there are, it still feels exposing to come out to them, because you are essentially sharing what you find hot. You are telling them what turns you on. I don't know about any of my family members' kinks and fetishes, and Uncle Dave, if you're reading this let's keep it that way. My straight female friends have never had to sit their mum and dad down and explain that they can only really reach orgasm if they are in a reverse cowgirl (thanks to

More magazine for the lingo) but if you're gay you basically have to tell your family and the rest of the world how and who you'd like to shag.

Sexuality isn't only about sex. It's about what kind of person you want to spend your life with, what identity you feel most at home with. Yes, I am a lesbian but I am lots of other things too: a wife, a mum, a daughter, a comedian, a football fan (the women's game, obvs), a friend, someone who loves to host dinner parties and have wine-fuelled deep-and-meaningfuls at midnight, a Lego and board-game enthusiast and so much more. But it sometimes feels like coming out reduces your existence to *only* your sexuality. I have spoken a lot about my sexuality; I even do a podcast about being out but I really hope one day I don't have to. If we had genuine equality I wouldn't have to make a podcast normalizing our experiences. It's the podcast I wished I had growing up. I am genuinely making it for teenage me because I didn't know that there were happy gay people in the world, just living their lives. All I had were sad, fictional Victorians, pining and hiding their love away.

'You can't be what you can't see' is a phrase attributed to Marian Wright Edelman, founder and president of the Children's Defense Fund. She believed that children are less likely to be hopeful for their future if they don't have role models to look up to that represent them. It's now a phrase used by many marginalized communities to encourage visibility and inspiration.

I have been told in the past that I have too much material about being gay, often by a man with 'generic name eight numbers' as their Twitter/X handle. But often the material isn't 'about being gay', it's about my life experience. Straight stand-ups don't get the same response when they talk about dating, marriage or family life but it seems for me some people will see it as pushing a lesbian agenda. And any lesbians reading this will know the main lesbian agenda is finding a quicker way to break in Doc Martens, getting Sarah Paulson and Jodie Foster to do a movie together and bagging tickets to a Brandi Carlile tour.

Coming out to my friends from drama school was one thing. Telling my parents was a lot harder – whilst their reaction was good, it took them a while to get their heads around it. We had to navigate their fears: that I would have a harder life, that they felt they didn't really know me any more. It was upsetting for all of us that they felt I'd been lying to them up until now and were a little betrayed by that – when in actual fact what I'd done by coming out to them was let them even further into my life. My cousin Jodi and my Aunty Jak were enormously supportive during this period and it didn't take long before my mum and dad were – as they always are – my very biggest supporters.

But telling my nan, possibly being rejected by her, was one of my biggest fears. In the end, though, there were months – a year even – when everyone knew except Nan. It became an enormous pink elephant in every room we were in. I just couldn't bring myself to do it. In the end Aunty Jak did it for me. She's strong and direct and could see that the fact we were keeping a secret from Nan was what was giving my mum the most trouble.

Jak rang her and said, simply: 'Suzi is gay and Ann [my mum] is worried about what everyone is gonna think and especially worried about your reaction.'

Nan called me straight after and said: 'I know now and I love you just as much as yesterday.'

It was one of the great phone calls of my life.

I know that not everyone's story ends like mine. I know people who have faced hatred and harm from the people that brought them into the world, from the people who are supposed to protect them. I am acutely aware that if I had been born a few decades earlier, coming out might have been totally inconceivable to me. I might have lived a closeted life, never truly knowing myself. This is why we still have Pride and why for many in our community our chosen family holds just as much love (and sometimes more) than the family we were raised by.

Once it – well, I – was out in the open, everyone released a collective breath. There was peace. It was done. I was still me, Nan was still Nan and we could all just go back to eating cheese sandwiches around her tiny table while sharing a packet of crisps.

I can't help but question what hiding so much of myself actually did to my body and brain. Was it the reason I have a problem with a disc in my back? Was part of why I couldn't concentrate at school because the burden of my sexuality loomed so large in my mind? And the puking didn't only happen in my twenties. I have memories of being fourteen and waking in the middle of the night to throw up. I later realized it happened when I was dreaming about women. I had literally disgusted part of myself so much I had to vomit. But *was* it disgust? Or does hiding who you are literally make you sick?

· · ·

I talked to Owen O'Kane, psychotherapist and bestselling author of *Ten to Zen: Ten minutes a day to a calmer, happier you*, about what it means to live an authentic life, and what happens when you don't.

'Every piece of research out there at the moment is clear, crystal clear, that you can't really differentiate physical and mental health.' Owen is clear too, and very calm, as he answers my first question. And with more than twenty-five years' experience in the field, and being a former NHS mental health clinical lead, he definitely knows his stuff.

'There's a clear pathway between the two. You talk about feeling sick, and we know that there's a close relationship between the gut and mind. It's a dual carriageway. When we're thinking about treating depression we get fixated on serotonin levels and some scientists estimate around ninety per cent of serotonin is produced in the gut.'

I never consider my gut when thinking about mental heath but it makes so much sense – shame can exist all over the body.

'You carry that stuff around with you,' Owen agrees. 'And if you're psychologically overburdened then you're going to be physiologically overburdened, too. The body carries that weight so the short answer is one hundred per cent yes, living a lie *can* actually make you sick.'

Shame has always been a recurring house guest for me. I wonder how much of an impact it has had on my overall mental health.

'Shame underpins a lot,' says Owen. 'Anxiety, depression, OCD, health anxiety, panic disorder, trying to control food, addiction; more often than not, if you dig deep enough, what you'll find is some degree of shame or humiliation that's never really been processed. And, particularly when it comes to sexuality, disgust and shame can be very, very close.'

When I think of myself in that ABC cinema, watching *Titanic* over and over again, I do remember feeling totally disgusted.

'I've never once, in my entire career, met a gay person who didn't have shame in their narrative in the background. When we look at it broadly, to be a queer person means to have experienced some degree of shame. It would be almost impossible not to. We live in a world where tolerance for difference is still a struggle for some people. So it's normal that you felt, or are even still feeling, that. But that doesn't mean that *you're* wrong or that *you're* a problem.'

Owen is also gay, and I wondered about his coming-out experience, having grown up in a very Catholic part of Belfast in the 1990s. I have a small insight into what it may have been like from my Catholic school but I imagine it was a lot more intense for him.

'Where I grew up there were churches pontificating and shaming and saying that if you do this you will go to hell.' It's hardly surprising that, like me, Owen tried to hide who he was. But whereas I chastised myself for years for not dealing with my sexuality sooner, Owen has a different view.

'Be kind to yourself,' he says. 'And be fair. You probably *had* to hide your sexuality from both others and yourself. For that period of time, it was a means of survival.'

Before Owen came out he spent three years in a monastery. I wondered how that affected confronting that part of himself?

'I had the best three years in the monastery. My motivation at the time was genuinely to do good in the world but in hindsight it probably enabled me in part to avoid my sexuality as I wasn't ready.'

That experience must have shed some light on anxiety, too.

'I remember one day, I came out of the monastery and was going home. I had a panic attack for the first time in my life. I now see that that panic attack in my early twenties came because I couldn't keep the secret any longer. There was no space to breathe. I couldn't hold on to the shame any more.

'I say in my book that shame can't survive fully when you bring it out into the light. And I do believe that to be true. Anxiety almost does us a favour, because it can act as a push, helping you get back to a place of balance and equilibrium. When anxiety starts to kick in it's saying: this isn't balanced, something has to change. And if you listen to your anxiety and work with it, if you're open to what it's trying to communicate, when it comes to shame, it's inviting you to bring it out into the world.'

While it's depressing to think that so many queer people share these feelings – even if it's clear they manifest in different ways – it's a comfort to know that I am not alone.

But I'm thirty-eight now. Surely it's about time I let go of these feelings from the early noughties. I need to chuck this shame in a box with some boot-cut jeans, a Furby and my Von Dutch cap and throw them on the bonfire. But according to Owen, that's not always so easy.

'I don't think there's a finite point where you ever completely get over shame. And that goes right across the board, when hurt and wounds happen. I don't think there's ever a point where they are completely and utterly healed because that's part of the human condition. It's not about believing you can completely heal shame. But what you can do is form an entirely new relationship with it.'

OK, I can get on board with this. In the same way I grew to love my tiny boobs, maybe my shame can become less of a burden to me.

'It's about accepting that you did feel shame, it's part of you, even if that's something you find difficult, and no wonder. Most people want to align with the parts of themselves that they feel proud of. They want the success, the glory, the being in love, the parts that are applauded and that we think will get us validated and accepted. Very often, we then alienate the other parts. But they're all elements of the human experience. Good therapy is about helping someone to see that they're made up of *all* of these parts.

'You don't get the highs without the lows. That's why I think so many queer people have such an affinity with Pride. I get really angry when I hear people say, why is there gay pride? You know, why don't we have straight pride? The reason you don't have straight pride is because you can't be killed because of who you are in a number of countries throughout the world for being straight. You will not experience discrimination based on your sexuality. Pride is the opposite of shame. And one reason we have Pride is because most queer people know what shame feels like.'

I agree, it infuriates me when idiots make comments about not having a straight pride. For a long time Pride to me was just about having a rainbow-coloured piss-up but as I have got older, become more politically engaged, and since I have become a parent, Pride now means a lot more. It means the fight for equality is ongoing, that we as a community and our allies are coming together to prevail over prejudice; it also sends a message to people struggling with their sexuality, and those across the globe where there are laws around homosexuality, that there is hope and understanding and compassion.

Before I ended our chat I wanted to know, after a career in psychology, having such a deep understanding of shame and anxiety, alongside his lived experience as a gay man, whether Owen had any advice for coming out. I know there might be people reading this book who are on their first step of that journey.

'One thing I think is important is to never force people to come out until they're ready. And until they're at a point where they know their lives better than anyone else. And if they know that they're going to be potentially rejected by family and friends and churches and cultures or whatever the context may be, they then have to be really mindful of what that looks like for them.

'And they may then have to make some psychological tweaks or adjustments to help them cope. There's a danger, if someone pushes themselves and they're not ready, and the people around them are not ready, that it can be really destabilizing. If I'm working with someone and I know they're about to come out and they're wobbling, my work would be to say OK, let's steady your own internal platform first. This is so that if things do go wrong or the reactions are not what you'd like them to be, that actually you're self-assured enough to know that you can manage, and that you don't need that validation or you don't need their acceptance.

'Sure, you'd *like* to have it. It would be lovely if we all lived in a world where everyone could love and accept you for who you are. But the world we actually live in means sometimes we have to adjust to the fact that not everyone is able to do that. And try to understand that that says more about them than you. My argument is, if you can't love somebody unconditionally, well, then you aren't loving them fully in the first instance.

'So to someone who's thinking of coming out, I'd say: steady your own platform first. Be at ease with it, do the work on that voice of shame that might come up when faced with others' judgements. It took *me* a while to do this but if we look at the fact that there are millions of us on this planet who have been created the way we are, and the way we are doesn't fit into norms, that doesn't mean that it's wrong, or that it's bad, or it's disgusting, or it's sinful, it just means that we're different, and difference can be incredible.

'And if we look at the lives of many queer people out

there, if we look at the colour and the joy and the variety that they bring to life. You know, there's no arguing that queer people add colour and space to life. And isn't that an amazing thing to be?'

Yes, Owen, I think it is. I wish I could have met Owen when I was wearing that tabard sitting on a box of salt-and-vinegar Walkers, reading a trashy article about Portia de Rossi. What I would have given to have heard such positive things about queerness. In making my podcast 'Out', I encourage listeners to write in with their own coming-out stories and while everyone has their own specific and unique journey there are frequently parallels across our stories, the shame, fear, feelings of being less than; but amongst the stories from listeners and interviewees, there is always hope, always triumph, always bravery. I know I could have had a relatively happy life with Simon but that wouldn't have been fair on him or me. I would have missed out on huge sections of who I am. I wouldn't have got to know what true courage means, I wouldn't have got to learn that my friends and family love me unconditionally, I wouldn't have met the wonderful queer friends and allies who share my community with me. I wouldn't have fallen in love with my wife. The route to get to this place of pride was a bit of a roller coaster for me, including occasionally getting off to chuck my guts up, but I am so pleased I went on it.

CHAPTER 4

Was Miley Cyrus right, when it comes to your career is it all about the climb?

It's a Saturday morning in 2008, and I'm mopping the piss-soaked floor of a men's bog. Before I started this job, I hadn't known how much damage could be done to a toilet with just the human body as a weapon, but it really is remarkable. The urinals smell like day 164 of a festival, the kind of smell that catches in your throat and threatens to cause breakfast to make a surprise encore. The tiles are cracked and veined with mildew. The floor is strewn with loo paper. There's a suspicious brown stain on the wall beside a frankly optimistic condom machine.

It wasn't meant to be like this.

At drama school, after I'd just about covered the astronomical cost of living in London, any leftover pennies from my bar job would go toward theatre tickets. Most Mondays, students could get cut-price tickets to some of the best venues in the capital: the National, the Royal Court, the Almeida. The seats were more often than not dreadful, a restricted view of only half the stage or being so high up

that altitude sickness was a genuine concern. I adored the
theatre and while many of my pals were working out how to
get noticed by a TV or film casting agent, I just wanted, to
use an unbelievably thespian phrase, to tread the boards. In
the last months of my training I convinced myself a career
as a theatre actress was waiting in the wings.

I graduated in 2007, just months before the financial crash
of 2008. After training forty-five hours a week for three
years, learning Chekhov, Shakespeare, Meisner, Stanislavski,
I left drama school with no agent and no auditions. Some
of my friends were in the same boat, but others worked
straight away, booking tours, little telly roles or West End
shows. All I had was a full-time job in a rough pub at the
dodgy end of Wandsworth (to quote *Love Actually*).

The clientele was . . . varied. From lunchtime most days,
a few regulars would be propping up the bar: skinny, frail
men who looked a lot older than their age, teeth like a row of
condemned houses, not a full set between them. They were
angry with the world, and, occasionally, also with me when
I took too long to pour their Guinness. They'd sometimes
snap, seemingly for no reason, and give me an earful on
feminism, the Labour Party or immigration (never positive,
obvs), which meant that even when they *were* friendly it still
felt a little threatening. The afternoons would drag, just me,
the old boys and people drinking to forget their lives outside
the pub.

Daytimes weren't busy, but I used the time proactively,
writing letters to agents. I spent hours researching their
clients, taking the time to personally, lovingly, *pleadingly*

tell them why I would suit their agency, and how it was worth them putting me on their books. I diligently wrote a handful every shift, and put them in the letterbox before the last post.

At around 6 p.m. the vibe changed. The old boys stumbled out and were replaced by a group of entitled, gilet-wearing lads, slick with Brylcreem, apparently allergic to saying please or thank you and, as the night wore on, increasingly hard work. The pub was opposite two rival estate agents, both of which were bold enough to ruin a nice car by wrapping it in a logo. Confusingly, the girls who worked with them seemed to find their behaviour charming. Come on, girls, have some self-respect! Surely no one could actually have found Hugo funny.

By 10 p.m. we were rammed. There'd be a constant stream of people at the bar. Some nice, some rude, all drunk. There *was* a customer code of conduct but it was lacklustre at best, mainly because the landlord had a nasty cocaine problem, so nasty that drug dealers were often lurking around demanding to know where he was. Usually, that was hiding in the kitchen, vowing to himself to make better life choices in future.

I would walk home at gone 1 a.m. after my shift, shoes sticky, eyeliner smudged, knackered from a double shift with a half-an-hour break (which I now realize was definitely illegal). I'd search my iPod mini for something to unwind to. The original cast recording of *Blood Brothers*. That'll do nicely. It had been seven years since I'd seen those Pink Ladies laughing at the stage door of a West End theatre and

I couldn't have felt further away from them or from Theatre Land. I wrote more than a hundred letters to theatre directors, theatre companies, casting directors and agents with my baby-faced headshot and a drama school resume, which, I was rapidly learning, meant nothing in the real world.

After not a single one of those letters got a reply, I knew I had to do something else. My anxiety was through the roof and eczema had spread across my hands, elbows and face from worrying about what I was going to do with my life. My skin is always my anxiety giveaway. Eczema even spread to my eyelids. It was so dry it would sometimes crack, I'd scratch it and then it would bleed. Fit! My first proper girlfriend, and dear friend for life, Faye, could see I was struggling and she suggested I give stand-up a try until some acting work came my way. I'd performed and written funny monologues before. Why not make the leap into comedy? As a teenager I'd watched French and Saunders religiously, and loved Victoria Wood – I can still quote large portions of *Acorn Antiques*. I saw Lee Evans at the Portsmouth Guildhall when I was fourteen. I remember thinking: I can't believe that small man (I was quite far back) is making all these people laugh, at the exact same observation, at the exact same time. It felt like a superpower. He was hilarious and he must have had an impact because more than twenty years later, my physicality on stage has been likened to Lee's in countless reviews. It ignited something in me which had then stayed dormant until the moment of Faye's suggestion.

I'd recently, thank goodness, got a new job in a much nicer pub, the Waterfront in Streatham (nowhere near a body of water). They ran a monthly comedy night which I always worked, and, the following Thursday, I arrived for my shift with a real spring in my step. I told Rich Wilson, the resident MC, that I wanted to give stand-up a go but I didn't know where to start. Very kindly, he took a copy of *TimeOut* from his bag, opened it to the page advertising London open mic nights and explained how to get on at the gigs. By the end of the following day I'd booked myself ten over the next four weeks.

My first ever gig was at a pub in King's Cross. The night was appropriately called the Lion's Den. It was held in the pub's basement; there was a small stage area with a couple of very worn, dubiously stained sofas either side, a mic stand held together with gaffer tape and a smattering of audience members. I was incredibly nervous. I didn't eat all day. When my name was called, I tried to appear confident as I walked up to the stage and took the mic off its stand. I can't remember anything about the gig itself – possibly I have blocked it out – except the rush of making a few people laugh. It was the kind of rush that's usually reserved for falling in love, skydiving or class A drugs. I knew straight away that I had my new obsession, I needed that feeling again.

But when you start out in comedy, gigs are tough. My first shows were the hardest I ever did. Open mic nights don't take place in purpose-built comedy clubs: they're usually in a small, soulless room above a pub, with a mic that doesn't work and an audience in single figures. You might be on with as many as ten other brand-new comedians and generally the standard is . . . low. One joke works, the next dies on its arse and as a newbie you've no idea why. It takes years to learn how to write material, perform it, to work out your onstage persona, how to link stories together, how to have the confidence to pace yourself and use silence. I didn't have any of those skills yet, and back in 2008 the open mic circuit was a horror show. It was a riot of misogynistic, hateful material with gags about rape, paedophilia and murder par for the course.

'Do you think women are funny?' is a question that every female stand-up from my generation or before has been asked by a journalist, critic or audience member. Or they've had the prickly, problematic 'compliment': 'I don't usually like female comedians but you actually made me laugh.' In my experience, the people who make these comments rarely see live comedy. I realized early on that every time I went onstage I was representing whether women, the whole 52 per cent of the population, could be funny. The lads I came up with never had to face that. It was clear right from the start of my career that, if someone sees a male stand-up tank, they might say: 'Oh, he was a bit rubbish,' but if a female stand-up has an equally bad gig she confirms their bias: women just aren't funny. It wasn't only the men in the audiences saying this stuff either. I found it particularly surprising when it came from women. I'd always think: don't you have a laugh with your friends? Don't you ever laugh so hard with the girls that you double over, genuinely concerned you might actually wet yourself? No? Maybe you need to get new friends.

My foray into open mic nights was the first time I'd heard that some people believed there was a disparity in humour between the sexes. It was news to me: my mum's funny, my aunt makes me laugh, my female friends are the most hilarious people I have ever met. And there was very little camaraderie from the more experienced comedians. I was once introduced by a male compere with: 'I'm sorry to say we have a woman next but I've heard she is actually not that bad. Please welcome Suzi Ruffell.' What hope did I have?! I was heckled before I'd even reached the mic. Because of all this fuckery, back then, as soon as we went onstage, female comics always had to work that bit harder to get a room onside. We were dealing with an assumption, even before we said our opening line, that we weren't as good as the boys. I'm glad to say this has improved a lot in recent years, with women like Jo Brand, Jenny Eclair, Gina Yashere, Sarah Millican, Sara Pascoe, Katherine Ryan, Kerry Godliman and countless others kicking down the door so now everyone has heard of funny female comics.

Even though I loved it, my anxiety was off the charts. I was so desperately nervous all the time I lost more than a stone in my first year of stand-up. I'd wake up with a start from nightmares of being in an enormous theatre and having thousands of people booing at me, but giving up never crossed my mind. The highs of a good gig were too sweet. When it was going well onstage I felt invincible, more confident than I ever felt offstage. I was constantly chasing that high. Having a great gig in a busy room is utterly exhilarating. Sometimes, it feels you can do no wrong. I made all these new comedy friends and I loved feeling that I was part of a gang. I was in love with the *idea* of being a comedian, too, always having my notebook on me, drinking coffee and smoking fags while noting down ideas and stories, travelling home from a gig late at night.

But if the highs were high, the lows were ocean deep. A bad gig feels like time is actually slowing down. You notice faces, expressions, you see the audience wince as they decide they hate, or worse, pity you. The air goes horrifically dry and, I don't know if this is just me, but my bum hole seems to flinch. As if even my bum is trying to escape the shame of being me.

But I didn't care. I gigged at least five times a week, sometimes as many as eight times, with double shows at the weekend. I had a pink fixed-wheel bike that would ferry me from Kennington to Hackney, from Tooting to Hammersmith. I would compose new bits on the way to gigs; arriving flustered and knackered helped get rid of some of the nervous energy before I got onstage. It's worth noting that, whilst I do lean towards obsession, this isn't especially unusual for new comedians. I didn't take holidays because I never wanted to say no to stage time; I gigged Christmas Eve and New Year's Eve. I missed weddings, funerals, birthday parties: nothing came before stand-up. It cost me friendships and relationships but I didn't care. I loved it. Being a success was more important than anything. I went at comedy with an ambition usually reserved for footballers heading to the World Cup. Just instead of one of those chic England tracksuits, I had skinny jeans, an oversized jacket and more eyeliner than the entire audience of a Good Charlotte concert.

It was clearly about so much more than just stand-up. Years later in a therapy session I would make the realization that so much of my ambition is because I always felt my sexuality had disappointed my parents, and giving them something to be proud of was my main driving force. It was another reason I'd been so determined to go to drama school and now that hadn't worked out, stand-up comedy *had* to. I wanted them to have something to tell their friends about. I felt they had given me such a lovely childhood and that, somehow, coming out was throwing that back in their faces. In a therapy session a few months after that I would eventually admit my sexuality was also a disappointment to me and my ambition was, in part, also about convincing myself I was worthy of success, love and friendship.

Before I go on, I want you to know that I am no longer disappointed about that part of myself. I will talk more about that in the chapter about falling in love. But I just needed you to know that I love my gayness these days, I love that I am part of a rich and diverse history and community and I trust my parents love me for exactly who I am.

One evening, about eighteen months into comedy, I went to the open mic night at the Comedy Café in East London. I'd had a pretty good set and as I made to leave I was stopped by Flo, an agent at comedy powerhouse Off the Kerb. She gave me her card and told me to get in touch. I'd been approached by a few agents in recent months but I was holding out for Off the Kerb. I felt that stand-up was 'my calling' – which is a dramatic way of saying I really wanted to make it my job. My vivid imagination was in overdrive. I'd picture myself on *Live at the Apollo*, playing West End theatres, sitting on chat-show sofas. It's worth pointing out, at this stage I had about fifteen minutes of hit-and-miss material, but I *had* to believe it could happen, otherwise what was all the hard work for? I was still very green but I knew I was getting better all the time. I was determined to really make it as a comic and I knew that Kerb – unlike the other agencies I'd been approached by – ran gigs all over the country so signing with them would mean more stage time, *professional* stage time, so more opportunities to improve. They looked after the likes of Michael McIntyre, Lee Evans, Jack Dee, Sean Lock, Jo Brand, Alan Carr and countless other stand-up megastars. The following week we met for a coffee and shortly after, Flo signed me. I couldn't believe it. I was delighted to be the smallest name on their website. And Flo got me more gigs than I could dream of. I performed everywhere, often driving more than a six-hour round trip to do a ten-minute set but I was finally on pro line-ups – so there was a paying audience that wanted to be there and assumed I was a professional too. I loved it. Off the Kerb got me enough work that I could jack in my day job (by this time I was a truly dreadful PA – the combination of ADHD and dyslexia wasn't ideal for a job that relied solely on organization) and I became a full-time stand-up comedian.

Maybe it was finally getting that ever so small taste of success, but during this period, for one of the first times ever, my anxiety mellowed. I had a plan. All I had to do was write material and gig as much as I could. Obviously I would occasionally die on my arse and fear that Flo was going to drop me. I'd have to ring and tell her.

'Rough one last night, Flo, I'm really sorry.'

But she was amazing.

'Don't be sorry, just get back onstage again tonight.'

Phew. Having someone in my corner, someone who believed in me, was a huge help. With stand-up, the only way you can really progress is by having a willingness to fail. Maybe that's true of all endeavours.

I've always loved Alan Carr's stand-up. For Christmas that year my brother bought me his first book, which is all about how he became a comedian. It was thrilling to be newly represented by the same comedy management as he was, and going to the gigs he was writing about. I downloaded the audiobook too, and there were sections I'd listen to again and again, travelling to shows around the country.

The next step up from open mic nights, and where I really cut my teeth as a stand-up, are the small comedy clubs dotted around the UK. The atmosphere was always boozy and some of the clubs were pretty rough – full of stags and hens that wanted the show to be about them. You had to make them laugh and quickly, if you had any hope of surviving your twenty-minute set. There would only ever be one female comic per show. The idea of two being on one bill was so rare it was basically unimaginable, which meant the dressing rooms were a sea of testosterone. Not only did I want to impress the audience and the booker but I wanted the grown-up comedians to think I was funny, too. Whilst the environment was somewhat hostile, I knew it was my only way to improve and the only way I could make a living from comedy, so I learnt how to do it. And I reached the stage where I thrived in rough rooms. I felt far more at home in a shady comedy club than at an arts centre or upmarket theatre.

I also had to take any gig I could to make ends meet. Taking on a creative career is a huge privilege. I am enormously lucky that I was able to give it a go and I always knew if things got really tough, I could move back in with Mum and Dad. But it was still a real slog. I'd drive hundreds upon hundreds of miles every single week: Cardiff, Newcastle, Lancashire, Brighton. I worry I have played a significant part in the climate crisis.

But it was so exciting just to *be* a working comedian, on the road, getting terrible night's sleeps in budget hotels. It would just be me, the truckers, and I assume murderers bedding down in a roadside B & B with the constant hum of a six-lane motorway just a stone's throw from my window. I'll admit, it did feel risky at times. I was twenty-five and travelling all over the country on my own, mostly in my car but also regularly by train, being on platforms by myself very late at night or nipping in to use the loo at a deserted petrol station. Nothing untoward ever happened, although I did once think a man was following me back to my car. I started running. He gave chase: 'Love!' he called. 'I'm not gonna hurt you. You left your phone!' It took at least twenty-five miles for my heart to return to its normal rhythm. I remember often feeling frightened and making a mental note to not tell Dad in case he tried to stop me from putting myself in potentially dangerous situations and therefore stop me from gigging. It definitely added some pressure and there were lots of girls who started out the same time as me and decided they didn't want to do comedy enough to justify feeling so vulnerable on the way home.

Luckily, the hard work was paying off and I was making progress all the time. But something I hadn't planned for was how much homophobia I encountered at gigs. 'I can fix you' is probably the heckle I've received most, shortly after coming out onstage. I'm never sure if I *need* to come out to an audience – my hair, clothes and general vibe scream 'lesbo' – but it's often good to let the audience know, so we are all clear from the get-go. When I was interviewing Canadian comedian Mae Martin on my podcast 'Out', we both said we preferred to get a gag in about our appearance and sexuality in the first few moments of our set before anyone in the audience would shout about it.

The first time 'I can fix you' happened, it stopped me in my tracks. I didn't know what to do. I tried to laugh it off but cried when I got back into the green room. An older comedian told me I had to get some 'put-downs' ready, as it was bound to happen a lot now I was playing the 'proper comedy clubs'. He took one look at my blotchy red face and told me I needed to 'toughen up'. He did not check if I was OK.

Over the years I've got better at dealing with it and looking less hurt. The most recent time was at a tour show, just a few years ago, on the outskirts of Bradford.

I was surprised because you assume when someone buys a ticket to spend an evening watching you specifically perform – as opposed to going to a general comedy night – that they've at the very least had a cursory google. About three minutes in, a man shouted: 'What you need is a big cock.' I responded: 'Then I doubt you can help.' The room erupted and I got to feel very clever but I cried the whole way home; Bradford to London, that's a big cry. It's worth pointing out that whilst there are always a lot of queer people at my shows, most of the time more than half the audience are straight folk who like comedy and don't give a hoot about the sexuality of who's onstage as long as they're making them laugh.

Back to being on the road in 2012. I was becoming more and more consistent onstage and I'd started to have great sets in clubs. I could hold my own. I'd worked out put-downs for the homophobic heckles that had become routine, and that I'd sadly just accepted as part of the job. I was lucky enough to start booking support slots on other stand-ups' tours. I had a brilliant time opening for my dear friend Josh Widdicombe. I would always have pretty solid gigs, nothing to write home about but also never embarrassing myself. Slowly, I was getting funnier.

It could only mean one thing: it was time to take on the Edinburgh Festival. The biggest arts and comedy festival in the world, it's *the* place to get seen by the most important people in the comedy industry, and I put a lot of pressure on myself (so on-brand) to have a sell-out fringe and travel home with a nomination for best newcomer.

It did not start well.

A prominent comedy blog named my show – *Let's Get Ready to Ruffell* – as having one of the worst titles across the whole festival. There were 2,000 shows at the fringe that year. It felt like a bad omen, a fitting start to a dreadful month. I foolishly chose to do my Edinburgh debut the year London hosted the Olympics so while I watched friends in London go to sports events and parties I did a show every night to fewer than twenty people, some nights single figures. Let me tell you, the face eczema was in fine fettle.

I felt I didn't belong at the Edinburgh Festival at all. All the skills I'd learnt in rowdy comedy clubs were useless at a posh arts festival like this. I felt so much more out of place than I'd imagined I would, like the whole thing just wasn't really for someone with a background like mine, with no links to the arts. My family trade is selling lorries while wearing sheepskin coats. Dad came up to the festival and was totally bamboozled by it: 'Two thousand shows? They can't all be good. A lot of these people just need to get a proper job!'

As someone who bases so much of their self-worth on people's opinions, I was demoralized every day of the fringe and to make things worse I'd also recently been dumped. She was beautiful, a bit older than me and could occasionally be cruel and thoughtless about my stand-up. I remember once she said: 'Maybe you're just not good enough.' Her comment rolled around my head for the entire month. It wasn't even as if I got bad reviews. There was so little buzz around me, the critics didn't even bother to come. Buzz?

I couldn't even get a hum. I remember after that dreadful fringe of 2012 my dad wrapped his arm around me and said: 'Don't worry, Suz, one day it'll make a great chapter in your book.' Well, you can be the judge of that.

I came home gutted. I threw myself back into the rowdy rooms. What relief! I *was* funny. I kept working hard, gigging constantly, and, I hoped, getting better.

A long two years later, a glutton for punishment, I took another roll of the dice and went back to the fringe, with a new show and with what I thought was a much better title: *Social Chameleon*. I am less sure of that now. I'd gained so much more experience, and I was full of hope that it would open some of the doors that had felt firmly locked last time. But I had an almost identical experience. Low numbers, no critical acclaim and the feeling that everyone had it worked out except me.

I pledged to stick it out for the month, but decided that at the end of the festival I was going to quit stand-up. Maybe it was time for me to get a proper job. I got back to London and arranged a meeting with Flo. I cried in a Whole Foods, then we went to a yoga class. I cried in that too. It's almost impossible to cry without suffocating in a downward-facing dog but I managed it. I explained that I couldn't handle being mediocre. I wasn't tough enough for the knocks and disappointment.

The problem was, I had made stand-up my life. Like the fourteen-year-old determined to go to drama school, I had become obsessed with it. It felt like there was nothing outside of it for me. Every bad gig or mediocre review cut deep, far too deep for a normal person. It made me feel worthless. And whilst I knew, in principle, that I could move back in with my parents, I was also aware I didn't really have a backup plan. Lots of my pals in comedy had degrees, private education, plenty of family money to fall back on. Many had flats of their own, bought by their parents. I was quickly approaching thirty (which I know *now* isn't old) and I knew if I wanted to start a new career there was no time like the present.

Flo encouraged me to give it six more months. And then she gave me the advice that changed everything.

She was tentative about saying it. As my agent, it's Flo's job to advise me, to help me do the best job I can onstage and in my career in general, but I think she knew there could be some sensitivity about what she was going to say.

We were sitting in an independent coffee shop in Clerkenwell, near the agency office, when she told me that she'd started to think I wasn't quite myself onstage, and that I was writing what I thought people wanted to hear rather than what I wanted to share. She told me that when I was offstage I was funny in a quirky, vulnerable way. She reminded me of the confessional comedians that I loved – Maria Bamford, Josie Long and Victoria Wood – and suggested I try to be more unapologetically myself onstage.

She was right. It struck me that for the first five years of my stand-up career I'd been doing an impression of a stand-up comedian. I'd spent so much time watching and gigging with Josh, Joel Dommet, Romesh Ranganathan, Seann Walsh and countless other straight men that I had sort of adopted a persona onstage that was an impression of a male stand-up. I wasn't confident in my sexuality offstage so I couldn't be onstage either. I was scared to be myself in case no one liked me. Looking back, I can see that a big part of that was because there were so many days on which I didn't like myself either. The homophobia I had received at gigs didn't help but, in fact, some of my own material was borderline homophobic and at my own expense.

I'd assumed that's what people wanted. It turned out that rather than them judging me it was me judging them.

I finally started writing honest material about my feelings, my family, my failures. I started connecting to the audience in a way I never had. I started having great gigs. I was honest. It was liberating. It didn't matter if I was in a posh theatre in the Home Counties or a workingmen's club in Manchester, if I went on as me and made them laugh, we all had a good time. As the six months Flo had suggested came to an end, I felt inspired by stand-up in a way I hadn't since the moment she'd taken me on, years earlier. I'd even started tentatively talking about my anxiety onstage and I was surprised how many people connected with that. One night, walking back to my car after a show, a woman ran out after me: 'My daughter is just like you,' she confided. 'She's gay and she's such a worrier. I just wanted you to know we both loved you!'

Wow. It was working, Flo was right.

She booked me for a gig in Old Street where there was a secret headliner closing the show. I texted to find out who. She messaged me back: You're going to love this. It's

Alan Carr. Flo was well aware of how much I loved Alan. I couldn't believe I was going to be on a line-up with him. I might even meet him after. I made a mental note not to be weird. That night I was having a great gig when I noticed Alan had snuck in the back of the club and was watching from side stage. I heard him laugh. All I could think was: don't fuck up now, Suz! I did meet him backstage and he was as lovely as I'd hoped he would be.

The following day Flo called and said: 'Do you fancy opening for Alan all around the country or do you still want to give up?'

It seemed that as soon as I was myself onstage, unashamedly so, things started to take off for me. After my months on the road with Alan I again went up to the fringe but this time it was totally different. I took a smaller room, made the tickets as cheap as possible so I didn't price out people like me and I had the festival I had longed for. Over the next five years I got all the opportunities I could dream of, awards, critical acclaim, sell-out tours, an appearance on *Live at the Apollo*, a seat on a chat-show sofa.

While it would have been great to have been an instant success I'm pleased I went the scenic route. I am pleased I didn't have my moment in the sun when I was trying to be the kind of comedian I thought people wanted me to be. It reminds me I can only really truly succeed when I am unapologetically myself.

• • •

And who better to talk about the role of failure in success, than the incredible writer and podcaster Elizabeth Day. I've found solace and comfort countless times whilst listening to her podcast 'How to Fail'. It helped me realize that periods *without* success can actually be good for you.

'I don't think of failure and success as linear and/or binary terms,' she tells me, when we chat via Zoom on a sunny Wednesday in April. 'I feel that sometimes they can happen simultaneously and that life is shaded by each. So, Truman Capote said failure is the condiment that gives success its flavour.'

I liked that. Surely we all need a little seasoning.

'I think that having a period where you don't feel successful, and when you feel that you are failing professionally, that you are kind of making mistakes and trying to work out who you are in this particular world of work, does two things. One, it focuses and clarifies your ideas and your passions. You get to learn what you're really about and what you find stimulating and creatively inspiring. And the second thing it does is make you appreciative, which makes you grateful. And all of the studies that have ever been done on happiness show that being grateful is a huge part of that.'

I know I've been guilty of not being able to step back and appreciate what I already have in life. I've been so career-focused and bloody-minded that I didn't take a moment to be grateful for my health or my family or my friendships. This reminded me of a story my dad told me a little while ago. When he lost all his money (you remember in Chapter 1 when I was a very anxious seven-year-old) he had to go up to London to appear in court about his bankruptcy. He was so gutted. He'd worked for a long time to establish his career, to be the man with the nice car, to be someone who went abroad on holiday, and in what seemed the blink of an eye it was all lost for ever. Dad phoned his best mate John, presumably on a massive '90s mobile phone, and explained how everything was lost. His life was effectively over. John gave him some directions and told him to give him a call when he got to the location. Dad followed them, arrived, and rang back. John said: 'Roly, you're outside Great Ormond Street Hospital. Some of the parents in there are going through absolute hell. You've lost a few quid, but you've got a happy and healthy family.' Quicker than you could say: the car's been repossessed, my dad's mindset was altered for ever. A quick dose of perspective was exactly what he needed.

'[The harder] periods of my life have been so formative and so instructive because I learnt that I could get through them,' says Elizabeth. 'I've had periods at work that feel really like I'm trudging through treacle, times when, to me anyway, I've felt very unseen and unsure. But it taught me that those periods do pass in the fullness of time, and that you can take action to speed that up. And it's made me forever grateful for any attention that I do have. And I think that I found myself in those moments of feeling unseen and undervalued and unvalidated.

'Actually, whatever success I have had, has come in my forties. And that's been great because I know myself and I think it enables me to show up as myself in an authentic way. But I don't think I would have got there had I not gone through the difficult bits.'

Like many people my family refer to the 'difficult bits' as character-building. I remember thinking, after being passed over for yet another job: when will my bloody character be built? Especially when so much of your self-worth is wrapped up in your job, it's hard to see that getting a knock-back can be positive.

'They're right, I absolutely do think it builds character. I think that when you experience a failure, and all of the feelings and the sense of loss associated with failure – sometimes the grief that comes along with it too – and you manage to survive it, that in and of itself is a marker of how much strength you have. For me it is, anyway – a marker of how much strength I have that I didn't know that I had at the time. So the more you withstand, the stronger you can feel. And sometimes that's the *only* way it builds character because sometimes failure feels totally chaotic and unfair and it comes out of nowhere. I firmly believe that not only will it build your character, but it will teach you something meaningful in the fullness of time.'

I think disappointment and failure have made me more determined for success. Elizabeth agrees.

'I'm extremely competitive. It's something I work on with my therapist a lot, because I now understand that a lot of my competitive drive comes from fundamentally low self-esteem formed in childhood. I'm aware of that fact about me now, and I'm growing an acceptance for it. The competitiveness sometimes causes me heartache, but I'm also aware that it's given me an enormous amount of drive. So I'm incredibly grateful for it. It's helped spur me on. And I think disappointment is part of that competitive-ness. So if I've experienced a professional disappointment, for example where my book that I really believed in didn't get into the bestseller list, that's disappointing, as well as triggering my competitive impulses if a book that I feel is less worthy is in there, which happens all the fucking time. But disappointment is kind of necessary for me to process because, ultimately, it shows that I care. I really care about what I'm creating and that's a great thing. It's a great thing to care about your work.

'So I try and repackage disappointment as under-standing how much I care. And that means next time, I'm going to remember that feeling. And it might not be a question of doing anything differently next time, because the failure might have been due to circumstances beyond your control. But it definitely means putting in the same level of effort and attention and care. And sometimes it might mean changing your strategy. But if it does, that knowledge wouldn't have been there without the disap-pointment. So, if everything goes according to plan and everything's a wild success the moment you put it out there, there's no data acquisition and then there's no growth. You can't grow anywhere unless it's into the unknown, and the unknown sometimes feels scary and anxiety-provoking and full of potential disappointment, but you have to take the risk.'

And it does feel risky. But actually I think dealing with failures and disappointment at work and in other areas of life makes people more interesting, more resilient and even more compassionate. To me, the people who've only experienced the easy life have far less to offer and they are less fun at dinner parties.

'Yes, definitely,' says Elizabeth, 'because there's no depth to them. And there's probably also a fair amount of arrogance and entitlement and privilege, because they believe that their smooth, easy path through life is the general human experience. And so they've probably never had to have that many conversations with people who aren't like them. They've probably never had to confront the darkest recesses of their soul. And they've probably been consigned to live half a life. And I've dated some of them and they're much less fun and just much less soulful'.

'Life is about being aware of your darkness; about accepting and understanding it as well as about maximizing the light. One can't really exist fully without the other. Give me someone who's imperfect and flawed and who has been cracked and stuck back together with different-coloured glue. And that's so much more beautiful. Think of the stories they'll have. They'll have great stories. It's all about the kintsugi.'

Kintsugi is the Japanese art of repairing broken pottery with gold glue. As a philosophy it treats breakage and repair as part of the history of an object, something that makes it more beautiful rather than something to disguise. And to me that sounds perfect.

CHAPTER 5

How do you mend a broken heart?

'Love hurts' is an understatement. Sometimes, it punches you right in the mouth.

It's 3 a.m. on 30 October 2016 and I'm sitting alone on the floor of my Hoxton flat.

I'm partway through my second bottle of wine, the ashtray is full and I have been on her Facebook page for the last two hours. I'm desperately trying to work out where she is, what she is doing and why she doesn't love me any more. It's been a rough few months: I'm anxious, overbearing, needy. My eczema is red and inflamed, I am depressing to be around, and I've had a haircut so bad I appear to be single-handedly attempting to bring back boy-band curtains.

The flat no longer feels like home. It's still full of her. She only took one suitcase. She said she'd come back for the rest when she'd sorted somewhere to live. I have turned photo frames over so I can't see us smiling back at me from Budapest, Auckland and London Pride. It feels dramatic but I don't care. I *am* dramatic. I am so sad, I feel like I'm going mad. I feel fuzzy. If I close my eyes tightly enough I can hear the blood whooshing around my head. I should go to bed. I should clean my teeth, wash my face, drink two pints of water and take some pre-emptive paracetamol but I don't, I light another cigarette and pour another glass of red. My laptop briefly goes to sleep, and I see my reflection in the black of the screen. I am a mess.

A glimpse is quite enough of my own bedraggled face. I go back on to Facebook, and her page is full of us: over three and a half years' worth of photos. (This was when Facebook was really popular and we had no idea they were selling our data to rig elections and sell us products we don't need. It was a place for photos, witty updates and FarmVille – a simpler time.) I am combing through the evidence like DCI Fleming trying to uncover when she started losing interest. At what point did she know a whole lifetime of plans was coming to an end? I can hear people getting home from their nights out, struggling with the heavy safety door below my floor, drunk friends giggling and whispering as they pass my front door. I feel deeply lonely. At 4 a.m., a friend starts sharing photos of the Halloween party that I was meant to attend. I casually flick through and gasp.

She is there. She has gone to a party. A party at my friend's house. She is in the background of a photo, laughing, dressed as a sexy witch. She looks good. Surely she *isn't* good? I haven't properly slept since she left, three days ago. I check WhatsApp and see she went offline an hour ago. Where did she go to bed? I worry. I feel like I am somehow responsible for her. Surely, she'll realize in a couple more days that this was a terrible mistake? That the London town house, summers in New Zealand and a sausage dog called Karl are still her dreams?

Well, maybe they are, but in her version there is no me. I have been edited out of our imagined future.

I must have fallen asleep on the sofa. It's morning, and I'm woken by the buzz of the downstairs entrance, convinced it must be her. I press the little key button and hear the slam of the ground floor door. I check my face in the mirror. Not good. I hear someone directly outside my front door. I open it. It's Mum and I fall into her arms, wailing. She lifts me up, confirms I look truly dreadful and takes me back to the sofa.

My dad, usually the most confident man in any room, shuffles in, bewildered, looking at the banshee that was once his daughter.

He offers: 'There's plenty more fish in the sea.'

I tell him to piss off.

(Sorry, Dad.)

Mum has brought sandwiches. My mum deals in sandwiches, she's bloody good at making them and a proper sandwich is a thing of beauty in my eyes. A birth, a death, a hangover, a break-up, she's convinced a sandwich will help. She's a feeder. The speed at which she'll offer a sandwich when you arrive at her house is a long-running joke between my friends and I. Quickest ever? She offered one out the window before I had even turned the car engine off. So of course she has a selection with her: cheese and cucumber, cheese and pickle, ham and tomato. But I can't eat. I can't actually remember the last time I ate something.

I am simultaneously drunk and hungover. And now I am sobbing. Hot face, tears streaming, snotty, breathless, slightly hysterical. I feel like a child. I am so relieved to have my mum. But Dad can't take it, he mumbles something about work; there's a discussion in the hallway. Mum is staying. By dinnertime she must be so bored of the same conversation we have had all day. Like a broken record, I would start over and over again, revisiting every argument, every disagreement, analysing how her new friends didn't seem that keen on me, her need for space, the nights she'd got home at 5 a.m., and the crowd she'd met and seemed desperate to get in with.

As we – or rather, *I* – talk, it slowly dawns on me that she had been leaving for a while. I was too frantic, too swept up in my own life to notice. That is sobering. Was I so self-involved I hadn't realized the person I loved was falling out of love with me, right in front of my eyes?

Mum listens and offers advice and tea. Eventually I eat half a cheese-and-cucumber sandwich. To be fair to Mum it's bloody delicious.

I first met, let's call her Jane, at a comedy club where I was doing a show – what a meet-cute cliché. I was surprised she liked me. She was confident, attractive and flirty, very much one of the cool girls. She kissed me on the first date and I fell immediately in lust. It was the kind of full-force relationship that takes you by surprise and it made me feel like my whole life was a quirky London romcom. We immediately started spending all our time together. We become night owls, out for hours, always desperate to learn more about each other.

She was relatively new to London and I loved having the opportunity to show off my chosen home town: the best place to dance (Bethnal Green Working Men's Club), the best bridge over the Thames (Albert and Victoria, especially beautiful after dark), the best bagel after 2 a.m. (Beigel Bake, Brick Lane), the best theatre and music, more culture and events than you can shake a cockney stick at.

I had butterflies in my stomach at all times. I first heard the cliché 'the lesbian urge to merge' on *The L Word* and, now, with Jane? I felt it hard. I wanted to merge with her. Not only did I want to spend all of my time with her, I wanted to be like her, I wanted to have her cool confidence and sexy devil-may-care attitude. Maybe I wanted to be her? Jane would come to my gigs, and, afterwards, we'd go to G-A-Y late and dance until the early hours, then jump on a night bus home to get a few hours of sleep. Feeling guilty that she'd have to get up and go to work, and also not wanting to leave her side, I'd sometimes ride the Tube with her for an hour and walk her to her office door. I couldn't get enough. We quickly became a couple. She'd come on weekend gigs with me all over the country – Birmingham, Bristol, Manchester – and we stayed in some of the best Holiday Inns this country can offer; the decor never dulled the romance. Wherever we went we'd seek out the local gay bar. Jane had the confidence to make friends wherever she went. Gay men loved her. They'd always assume she was straight, then love her even more when they realized she was part of the gang. The next day we'd revel in sharing a hangover, something else that belonged to us as a twosome.

I didn't want to go anywhere without her. I felt great in her presence. I was fearless. I had poise, a boldness I had never felt before. She came to shows, friends' birthdays, dinner dates with my very best friends. None of them would bring their partners but I didn't care, I could barely see past Jane, and my new inflated ego.

My housemates, two friends from drama school, were suspicious. They felt we were taking it too fast, and, to me, seemed annoyed that she'd come in and upset our happy little home life. They told me, when I pushed them, that they thought I was always putting on a bit of a show for her, trying to be funny rather than just being myself. I brushed it off. They were straight, after all. How could they ever really understand the intensity of a relationship between two women? They could never get how exhilarating it felt to be in love, in actual love, with an actual woman when you'd spent so many years hiding that part of yourself away.

They'd regularly make subtle suggestions about taking it slower. On one occasion, they got home drunk and saw her shoes next to mine in the hall. I overheard them exclaim: 'Oh God! Why is she always *here*?' Maybe that one wasn't quite so subtle . . .

I didn't listen. Instead, I decided to move out.

I'd only known Jane for five months when I swapped my fun Vauxhall house share for a charming little garden flat in Archway. We put pictures on the walls, got a tiny kitten and made huge plans for our life together. That first year was brilliant. Everything was perfect.

As our relationship deepened, I never stopped being surprised that Jane liked me. Whenever we entered a room together I felt like shouting: look, everyone! One of the cool girls thinks I'm cool too! I was bowled over by her carefree attitude, how lightly she took on the world, how little she worried about the future. Her aim was simply to have a good night and deal with tomorrow, tomorrow. She was a free spirit, the type of person who can wear a beret without feeling like a prick. Whereas, being consumed by what others think of me, I regularly torture myself at 3 a.m. with memories of social missteps from years gone by.

The time I congratulated a woman who wasn't pregnant.

The time on the bus when I kindly offered to move so that the two older East Asian ladies could sit together, only to be told they didn't know each other.

The time I met Mel C, lost the ability to speak, stood in silence for what felt like a week, awkwardly muttered: you mean a lot to me, you always will, and shuffled away.

She had none of that: she slept soundly. Every single night.

I've always been jealous and, frankly, somewhat suspicious of people *without* anxiety. Do they have the answer to life? Have they worked it all out? Have they concluded that worrying doesn't actually fix anything so they may as well not bother? I do agree with that statement in principle. I am well aware that I've not yet managed to stop the climate crisis, solve inequality, or create a time machine to erase those aforementioned social gaffes during the sleepless witching hours, but the logical part of my brain doesn't kick in when anxiety takes hold.

My anxiety comes in so many flavours but freelancer anxiety is one of the worst. Sometimes I'm overwhelmed by the thought that all the work will dry up, all the comedy clubs will close and TV will stop being made. (It felt like another of my wildly imaginative nightmares until March 2020.) It is very easy to become a workaholic when you are a freelancer and to fetishize being consistently exhausted because your ambition is so great. Why would I give my only employee (me) a night off?

My desire to succeed has meant that I've never given myself much down time. I thought if I had too much fun I might miss an opportunity. I felt like I was in a race to the finish line, but it was a finish line that has turned out to be both imaginary and constantly changing. All my friends were also ambitious creatives so spending so much time with Jane, someone who was happy to just skip through life, forced me to slow down physically.

However, because my brain unfortunately belongs to me, it was impossible to slow down mentally. So, yes our mini-break in Budapest was nice but I spent most of it agonizing over why I didn't get booked for the new series of *8 Out of 10 Cats*. It must have been enormously tiresome trying to relax in the warm water of the Széchenyi Thermal Spa while your girlfriend stares at her phone willing a good-news email to arrive. A break away together should have been refreshing but my inability to stop talking or at least thinking about work meant the trip was doomed. My work preoccupation was the rub that became the blister which, eventually, caused our relationship to burst. For her, spending crumbs of time with someone who was not only obsessed with the next step on *their* career ladder but also where everyone else was on theirs was ~~probably~~ definitely exhausting.

It would be easy to cast Jane as a villain, the baddie who broke my heart and left me shattered, but she wasn't – she just stopped loving me. Her actual words were: 'I love you, I'm just not in love with you.' See? Not a villain, just a cliché. Today, with the benefit of time, I can see we were a terrible match. We didn't want the same sort of lives, we didn't value the same things.

What I really needed to do was spend time on my self-worth rather than be in a relationship that was moving too quickly and often made me feel panicked and low.

Quite early on in our relationship, someone told me I was 'punching' above my 'weight'. Such a strange way of describing someone being fit – she was so much more attractive her face would be in a higher boxing weight category. And I believed them: she was super-attractive and so I had to work on being hilarious all the time. I felt like that was all I had going for me. I needed to be 100 per cent great company, every single second, to keep her interested. (Turns out my flatmates were right after all.) It worked for a while, but it wasn't sustainable. I like nothing more than a night in, a box set about a female detective (ideally played by Suranne Jones) inspecting a body that has washed up on the beach of an eerie British seaside town. If you add a bag of Maltesers and a glass of Pinot Noir you've pretty much got my perfect evening, but she liked going out. She wanted to be around people and have fun. I can find people exhausting and fun overrated. And anyway what is more fun than a bag of Maltesers? Other than a family-sized bag of Maltesers?

The relationship was never easy. After that glorious first year, it always felt like hard work. I thought that's what relationships were meant to look like, though. Every film will tell you that there has to be triumph over adversity for it to be worth it. I thought easy equalled boring. I now realize easy might equal a boring movie but it's the sign of a happy, healthy relationship. Things that aren't those signs: a screaming match at 3 a.m. after her phone had died when she was on a night out and I'd (obviously) assumed she was dead (hello, old friend death anxiety). Constantly feeling like you aren't good enough for the relationship you're in so taking every throwaway comment or aloof text message utterly to heart. We would have dramatic arguments then emotional reconciliations and according to films that's what love was. At the time, I thought Jane gave me butterflies of excitement, but now I think it might have been my body trying to tell me: Beware! Danger! Things never felt peaceful with us, and I suspect that's what happens when you know in your bones you're on shaky ground.

But back in 2016, mid-heartbreak, I had yet to understand any of that. Maybe play some Adele while reading this next bit.

Mum stayed for a few days and good friends rallied around to help tend my little broken heart. And slowly, I began to understand that I wasn't only heartbroken about losing Jane: I also felt I'd lost part of me. The relationship gave me the kind of acceptance I'd always craved but never truly felt. On some level, Jane represented those cool girls at school that hadn't liked me.

What's more, I feared I'd lose our shared friendship group, the gang we went on nights out and holidays with. Jane said from the start of the break-up she wanted to stay friends, but then, that's always easier for the person who doesn't feel like their heart's been ripped from their chest and volley-balled across a motorway only to land in the slow lane of the M25 to be squished and bruised by a succession of heavy goods lorries on their way to a port on the final working day before Christmas.

In those first few weeks I bumped into her everywhere: parties, work drinks, our favourite coffee shop. Each time, it was devastating. I felt like I was being hollowed out with an ice-cream scoop. I was desperate to see her but when I did it was terrible. I cried in a *lot* of public toilets. I knew I missed her but it turned out what I missed even more is who I felt like I was when I was with her. She gave me the sort of self-assurance I had never managed to summon by myself. Throughout our relationship, I always felt grateful to her. I could never quite shake the feeling that she was slumming it with me. This created an imbalance early on which we never grew past. Of course, it's good to feel lucky to be with your partner, but it's important that you believe they're feeling lucky too.

I cried every day. Sobbing in a Marks & Spencer's next to a two dine for a tenner sign was a particular low. And I consumed everything I could about break-ups: books, films,

TV shows. I watched the whole of *Sex and the City* twice. I had to reassure myself there was life after heartbreak. I remember my friend Josh telling me that one day I just wouldn't feel sad any more and that I would fall in love again. I simply couldn't imagine it.

And perhaps I wouldn't have to: a month later, just as I was starting to feel vaguely human again, my phone pinged. It was a text from Jane: **Maybe we made a mistake.** My heart soared: finally she'd seen sense. I replied in seconds agreeing and within hours we were at the pub together. Still, I was campaigning for our wilted relationship, making her laugh, reminding her of our little in-jokes, trying to come across as cool, relaxed, changed even. Within a week she had moved back in but everyone (including, if I am very honest, me) knew it wouldn't be for long. You know how you're taught to not go back to a lit firework? Well, I did and it exploded in my face. Two months later her bags were packed again, and this time I knew it was for the best.

Strangely, it was something completely unrelated to Jane that made me realize it was over with her. During those two months in which we were back together, my beloved ninety-four-year-old nan was getting weaker and weaker. She'd been in and out of hospital, had lost her appetite, more than nine decades on this planet had made her body very, very tired. We were extremely lucky that her mind stayed sharp, so we all had the chance to say everything we needed to say, to thank her and let her go knowing she knew how loved she was.

It became clear that the end was coming closer. I was travelling to Portsmouth every couple of days, soaking up every moment I could with Nan. We had an especially close relationship. I like to think we had a particularly special bond, although I imagine her four other grandchildren feel like that too. I think it was her that was special. I hadn't been back to London for a few nights. Mum, Aunty Jakki, Jodi and I shared out time at Nan's bedside and one of us was there around the clock. She wanted to die at home and we didn't want her to be on her own when she did. One day, though, there was a ten-minute window between visitors and that was the moment she decided to leave. I think that's how she wanted it. She had a very good death, as deaths go, maybe even a great one: an old lady warm in her bed just like Rose in *Titanic*.

My heart shattered. The previous heartbreak I was dealing with paled into insignificance. A few nights before Nan passed I had laid in her bed next to her. She was drinking tea from a beaker cup in comfortable, loving silence, surrounded by pictures of our family. My gaze settled on a photo of her and Gramps on their wedding day. She had been a widow for twenty-six years by then. But every day she'd speak to his photo, not a full-on conversation, just a few words. It was like she wanted to keep him in the loop, let him know the big news: 'Oh, Jack, you should see little Brody, he was one yesterday. He is so lovely, you would've loved him, Jack.' She'd been missing her husband for more than a quarter of a century. And she was ready to see him again. She was totally at peace. She knew my relationship had been on the rocks for a few months and whilst she wasn't one to pry she did offer a few words of advice: 'Don't chase someone who doesn't want you. It'll never work. Wait for someone that really loves you.'

It was like Nan had turned the lights on. Of course it was never going to work with Jane. No great love story ever features the line 'when I convinced her to love me'.

The second time we broke up, it was actually a relief. Suddenly the bed which had felt too big and lonely just a few months ago felt just right for just me. That doesn't mean I was over it immediately; it was still difficult in many ways but it was good difficult. Like trying to write a book when you have ADHD and dyslexia and anxiety and occasional self-esteem issues. You've just got to keep pushing and hope on the other side will be something great.

Because we moved in the same circles, I knew I would hear if she started dating someone. One Sunday morning a couple of months later my phone pinged. I was feeling enormously smug because I had just smashed a CrossFit class and was high on endorphins and the holier-than-thou energy of being hangover free on the Lord's day. I was grabbing a coffee and casually flirting with the barista. She was new to my local coffee shop and I hadn't found out if she was gay and flirty or just European and friendly.

Have you and Jane broken up? the message on my phone screen read.

I don't want to get involved but she was with an actor I know at a party last night, I didn't want you to be the last to know.

I knew this text would come at some point. I bolstered myself for an emotional sucker punch, but it didn't arrive. I actually laughed, I don't really know why. I am not proud of the relief I felt that she'd gone for a guy after me. I am well aware that for many, many people attraction is not about gender but about the person. Bisexual folks might be tutting and shaking their heads but to be honest, truly honest, the fact that she wanted a man allowed me to remove some of the self-loathing and self-hate. And when you are putting the pieces of your heart back together you have to take the little wins where you can. If she wanted *him* that was beyond my capability. It felt less about me and that somehow made things easier.

There were other things, too. I had recently turned thirty. She was four years younger, and the age gap had begun to feel more like a canyon. My biological clock was ticking more and more loudly. I wanted to set down roots and start saving for the future. I had even suggested marriage at one point. I know these aren't things that everybody wants. I know that some people are very happily child free, that they don't feel the weight of expectation encouraging them to fall in line, but that's not me. I don't mind the weight of expectation. In fact, I like to have a plan. I knew I wanted a family long before I knew I wanted a wife. And that wasn't in her future, certainly not the immediate one. I had been trying to make a square peg fit a round hole for years. It was time to take my square peg to market, in the hope of finding a square hole – I regret this analogy but I'm sticking with it.

Having your heart broken is a humbling experience. In many ways, over the next six months I had to start all over again. Because our lives were so entwined and it was inevitable I would see Jane if I carried on as I had been, I didn't. I stopped going to the same parties and dinners, because whenever I bumped into her I seemed to stumble backwards in getting over her. So I leant on the friends who didn't know her and I tried to make new ones. More than anything I had to work out who I was now. Like a re-upholstery for the soul, the foundations were the same but it was up to me how to redesign myself. And I found, to my surprise, that there was something incredibly liberating about starting from scratch. I cut my hair – curtains be gone! I went to CrossFit and to yoga. I treated myself to some really expensive bedding. I bought some new outfits – she wasn't a fan of me in a suit. Friend, I bought a lot of suits.

I slowly started remembering the parts of myself I had rubbed out in order to be cool enough for the cool girl. I bought a Super Nintendo. I listened to musical theatre in the car, I sometimes listened to country music when I cooked. I left parties early. As always, I threw myself into work: and stand-up didn't let me down. I gigged constantly all over the country, telling strangers about my break-up, getting laughs of recognition, slowly feeling more like myself. As time wore on I started to like this 2.0 version of Suzi. She was more relaxed, more fun, probably because she wasn't always worried that her girlfriend was about to ditch her. Her leaving me was my greatest fear and when it happened I found a strength I didn't know I'd had. My friends and my mum propped me up and I feel lucky I got to learn how much I am loved by those people.

That happened eight years ago. I am writing this chapter from my office in my dream house in Brighton. Downstairs I can hear my daughter and wife laughing. I don't know what they are laughing about but the comforting hum of a happy home is all around me. What I didn't know when I was crying on the floor in Hoxton was that Dad was right, there were plenty more fish in the sea and my fish was on her way. The greatest love story was just around the corner. On reflection, I am grateful to Jane. We shared some good, nay, great times in our relationship. But she also held up a mirror to who I was: an intense and anxious workaholic who lost a relationship at least in part because she didn't make time for it. When I met my wife, Alice, I knew I had to reprioritize if I wanted love and a family.

The heartbreak of that relationship means that I am a better wife to Alice. Once you've cried – and I mean really sobbed – alone in a Pizza Hut on the outskirts of Birmingham, you are humbled, you have no choice but to look hard at yourself and work out what you really want from this life. I truly believe that having your heart crushed makes you more compassionate, more understanding and kinder. I am going to talk to bestselling writer and professional agony aunt Dolly Alderton about heartbreak and find out if she knows how to mend a broken heart.

· · ·

I have long been a huge fan of Dolly Alderton. I remember reading *Everything I Know About Love* on a bus and not being able to put it down despite the fact that reading whilst moving makes me feel very sick. When we spoke – she having been kind enough to give me some time right after her latest massive global book tour – between you and me, I had to try very hard not to fan-girl. Dolly's books often deal with love and heartbreak and I was desperate to know what she'd learnt from immersing herself in characters who were dealing with it. With many years having passed since my heartbreak with Jane, I can now see there were so many red flags, I might as well have been in a bullring.

I kick off by asking Dolly why she thinks we choose to ignore the signs when we're hoping and hunting for love.

'It's really as simple as this. It's quite rare to be physically and chemically and spiritually and intellectually attracted to someone who feels exactly the same about you, and to meet at the right time when you're both looking to connect to someone. It's rare. It's really rare. I was single in London for the best part of ten years. I know how rare it is. We can be excused for taking those opportunities and ignoring the things that may happen.

'I think that it's much harder to meet someone than people make out that it is.'

With Jane, I chose someone who ended up not wanting the real me, and so I tied myself in knots trying to be the version of myself that she did want. Since then, I've always thought that the fact I had to try so hard meant our relationship was always destined to fail, but Dolly has a different take.

'I think it totally depends on your disposition because, if you follow *your* argument, then true intimacy can only exist between two humans when you're bringing your whole selves, and are unafraid of showing all of who you are over a long period of time. And that, as you get to know each other and fall in love with each other, you stand before each other in your fullness and you accept each other. That's true connection, true love, flaws and all. And I do believe that, but I also believe this: that there's a certain type of person who comes alive in a romantic relationship, whether it's one date or fifty years in, by feeling like they're still pursuing their partner.'

It would be remiss not to acknowledge that we are all made up of different things and what we're looking for in relationships isn't the same, however disappointing that may feel in the moment.

'For me,' Dolly reveals, 'romance has always been a place of adventure. But I know for other people, it doesn't feel like that. What they want from romance is a sense of place, for it to feel like home. I think it's just about understanding yourself – understanding how you love and how you like to be loved.'

I wish I'd thought of this when I was in that state of deep, deep heartbreak. It's liberating to just accept that someone wants to love differently to you. It somehow makes it all feel less personal.

Doesn't change the fact, though, that being dumped can still be totally crushing. I ask Dolly if she agrees with my hypothesis that heartbreak makes you more compassionate.

'That's such a great question . . . I think it does, because when you've been through heartbreak, which I'm classifying as wanting so badly to be with someone you love, but, for whatever reason, you can't be, it's so painful. It almost feels like the violation of a human right, to not be with the person that you love. And of course, that's ridiculous, because the other great human right of life is that no one has to be with someone that they don't want to be with. And yet, when it happens to you, it's so all-encompassing and just so painful. But once you've been through it and you start talking to friends and family, you understand that this is something that touches every single person's life.

'We're the walking heartbroken. Everywhere you look, whether it's a man in his eighties or a teenager, the likelihood is they carry this experience with them. And you do have to carry it with you. It's not a trauma that you can discharge from your body. Because when someone loves you and you love them, they form the person that you are.

'So you have to carry that with you. You have to carry the memories of that relationship with you, which also means carrying the pain of the loss. And I think once you understand that this is something that everyone has been through, it certainly deepens your empathy, not only of people who are going through break-ups, but – and this will sound a bit overblown, but stick with me – of the human condition itself. Of what it is to love people, to lose them, and to find the fortitude to carry on living, and sometimes carry on loving again. It's so admirable, so brave and hopeful and amazing that humans just keep doing this. So, yes, I think heartbreak does give you a deeper connection to your fellow man.'

So what does Dolly think about the ultimate question. How do you get over it? How do you mend a broken heart? Can you? She grins back at me from the Zoom screen.

'OK, so I'll tell you when I understood fully how to mend a broken heart. It was when I was heartbroken a handful of weeks before lockdown, and it was an absolute whopper, this heartbreak. It wasn't a big relationship, it was a moment in time actually, but what I also now understand is that the depth and pain of heartbreak are often not correlated to the quality and length of the relationship. It's about what the relationship represented to you.

'So, I was going completely insane in those three months of lockdown. I was living on my own in the middle of nowhere. I soon understood how you mend a broken heart because all my tools were taken away from me. And that's why I think that it was the worst heartbreak I'd experienced. It was because everything in the first-aid kit was unavailable to me due to a global health crisis.

'And that first-aid kit is friendship, spending time with the people who know and love you, who crucially make you laugh.

'It's conversation, the conversation of processing what and analysing what has happened and the conversation of distraction, of hearing your friends' news, talking about the future, laughing about the same stupid shit you've been laughing about for decades.

'It's the conversation of hope, the conversation of future

plans, of what life will be like beyond the heartbreak, but also the conversation of who you were before. So, when you spend time with people who know and love you, who have known and loved you before this relationship, it's so important to bury yourself in the connection and the history of those friendships because they will bring you back to yourself.

'They will remind you of life before you met this person and therefore you will know that there will be life beyond them too. So that's the most important thing.'

This rang so true for me. It was not only when I remembered who I was before Jane but also when I embraced who I could be without the weight of a relationship destined to fail that I could grab life by the horns. When you get past the actual sadness you do find excitement for what is next or rather who is.

Anything else? I added because it's not often you get a one-on-one with a professional agony aunt.

'I'll be cautious about how I recommend this,' she says, 'because I know this isn't the same for everyone. But alcohol, for me, has been so medicinal for heartbreak. My perfect place is a glass and a half of wine, it doesn't really get better than that moment. It could be the apocalypse and the world could be burning down around me, and I'd find a way to make a joke about it. A glass and a half for me? That works.'

I have to say, I was unsure about keeping that in, because I know that for some people alcohol would be harmful in this situation or that addiction is something you might have struggled with. But in the interest of the extreme honesty which underpins this book, I'll say that I too have used alcohol medicinally. I'm lucky that for me it has been a gentle hug, or a light numbing of feelings too overwhelming to deal with – a way to make a long night a little more jolly.

'Distraction, too,' Dolly continues. 'Anything you can do to get out of your head – activities where you basically can't be on your phone stalking. Being outdoors, going on trips, trying something new, cooking something you love, listening to podcasts. Because I live on my own, when I'm heartbroken podcasts become this constant cacophony of just funny, warm people chatting because they can lift me out of my own overthinking.

'From thirty to thirty-four, I became just this accidental expert on heartbreak. It's an annoying thing to become an accidental expert on, but I just kept finding myself in this landscape, this rocky, dangerous, precarious, uncomfortable landscape. The circumstances, and the route I took to get there, were different every time, but then ultimately I'd call a friend and be like: I'm here again, I can't believe I'm here again.

'So I've accidentally spent a lot of time there over the last few years and I also now know how important the cold turkey method is.'

Dolly is emphatic on this point.

'You have to block them – you have to block them on social media, you just have to. It's so scary when you do it, but you have to, because otherwise you are still in a one-sided virtual relationship with them, which keeps them alive in your heart, which means you can't move on.

'And it means that, every day, your imagination is given small kernels of information that – with the *right* imagination and the *right* heartbreak and the *right* rage and sadness can just bloom into this floral extravaganza, this botanical extravaganza from this tiny kernel. And actually you never really know what's going on from their side.

'And also what does it matter?' she points out. 'You're not with them any more. So any information that you're trying to collect is useless, other than a method of torture. There's no point.

'One other thing that a friend said to me when I was heartbroken, when I was like seventeen, which I tell everyone now, is that you have to, in the first six months, starve nostalgia of oxygen.

'You can't romanticize. Your brain will be so ready to start romanticizing everything about your relationship and to forget all the reasons why it didn't work. And the most important thing you can do with that is delete your entire message history. The entire message history.

'You don't need these concrete things to obsess over, to remember it. You will remember it, so you have to just delete them from your life. And then, and then actually, once the pain subsides, you'll be able to remember stuff, new stuff. But you have to give yourself a chance of healing, and you can only do that by going full cold turkey.'

If you're reading this with a sore heart and considering a little peek at their Insta, block them right now, don't reread the messages from happier times and don't for the love of God watch one of the videos your smartphone makes with soppy music. Chat with your friends, make plans, if it's right for you have exactly one and a half glasses of excellent wine, and in six months when you're back on form, feeling on top of the world and frankly looking bloody fit, you can thank me (or rather Dolly).

CHAPTER 6

What does falling in love do to your body and brain?

Having my heart broken didn't stop me being a big romantic. I want to get that out of the way at the start of this chapter, as a notice, a signpost, maybe even a warning telling the cynical and joyless to just skip right ahead. (Although, let's face it, I probably lost those guys a good few chapters ago.) I watch romantic comedies. I cry at weddings. I always rooted for Ross and Rachel. I believe in love, the joy of it, the magic of it.

Epic, extraordinary, cinematic love is how I ended up here, after all.

When I was a kid I loved my nan's stories about her and my gramps during the war. In the early 1940s, Portsmouth was bombed relentlessly and I'd beg her to tell me tales of Spitfires flying over the city, of spending nights in the air-raid shelter, of soldiers in uniform coming home and heading straight for a pint at my great-gran's beer house. All this was the backdrop to the sweeping love story of Jack and Joan. In 1940 my grandfather volunteered for the war effort. Just weeks later he was called up as a Royal Engineer; he packed his bags and left for training. He and my nan, boyfriend and girlfriend in their early twenties, missed each other terribly, but that was their lot and they accepted it.

Deciding not to play by the rules, one night Gramps slipped out when no one was looking. He knew if he timed it right he could steal a few hours with my nan, so he watched and waited until the gates were unmanned. He knew the watchman would need a wee sooner or later, and when he did, out Gramps crept. He scurried down to the bus stop and waited. The bus took him thirty miles down the road and straight into Nan's arms. Of course, time ran away from the young lovebirds and by the time he returned to barracks, at gone 11 p.m., it had been noted he was missing.

He was promptly court-martialled for absconding and when his superior officer called him into his office and asked, frustrated: 'Jack, what the bloody hell am I going to do with you?', my gramps replied: 'Give me an afternoon off so I can marry her.'

And that's what they did.

Jack and Joan spent the first five years of their marriage apart: he was fighting the Nazis in Europe and she was fighting paper cuts in Portsmouth at a book-binding factory. Their only contact was by mail – she never had more than a few words on a postcard to reassure her he was still alive and to send his love. We later learnt that Gramps was enormously brave in the war. He fought all over Europe, was shot at countless times, ran into the sea in Dunkirk and managed to swim to the relative safety of a fishing boat. He travelled as far as Africa, caught diphtheria and malaria but all that was ever jotted down on those postcards was: *Darling Joan, I am safe. Sending all my love, Jack.*

When the war ended, Gramps sailed home from France on a naval ship. The owner of Nan's factory said all the women whose husbands were finally returning home could leave early to meet them off the boat. She and the other wives hurried to the docks just as the ship arrived. He disembarked with hundreds of other men and the dockyard rang with shouts, cheers and jubilation for the Pompey men who'd made it back. Couples everywhere held each other close, mothers gripped sons like they'd never let them go again, and Jack and Joan searched for each other in the crowd. She saw him first – clocked his tired, handsome face, and ran as fast as she could into his arms. He picked her up, spun her around and kissed her. He was home, he was safe and they could finally begin their married life. It lasted more than fifty years.

I used to ask Nan to tell me this story again and again. It sounded like a film: my grandparents had their very own real-life Hollywood moment. I'm sure their marriage wasn't always perfect, but by anyone's standards they absolutely smashed it, and for me, they set the bar pretty high.

Fast-forward over seventy years to 2017 and their grand-daughter is rating potential suitors on an app that encourages you to share your kinks. A pretty far cry from Hollywood . . .

I have fallen in lust more times than I'd care to admit, but real love, *Hollywood* love, that 'one' that my grandparents had, was a far tougher nut to crack. With Jane, I'd tied myself in knots, trying to be the person she wanted. After we broke up, I came back into myself. I was determined to be entirely me, and to find someone who liked the most honest version of me. It was time to start dating.

Some people love this activity. They see it as a sport, a numbers game, but, as I soon discovered, I wasn't one of them. I'd done so many auditions in my life that dates felt like more of the same. 'Hello, I'm here to read for the part of your life partner, would you like this in my own accent or RP?' I'd wonder if I'd get a recall. I might even land the role for a few months before my job made meeting up tricky to organize, or they'd get bored with me, or my relentless anxiety would find a way to throw a spanner in the works.

I think I liked the *idea* of dates more than dates themselves, and I did love the getting-ready part. When I still lived in my small flat in Hoxton, I'd put on my Pride Bangers Spotify playlist, tracks from Lady Gaga, Elton John, Queen, Diana Ross, and Tegan and Sara, all expressly chosen to get my confidence up, usually accompanied by an ice-cold glass of Oyster Bay. I'd shower, wash my hair, exfoliate my whole body and dress in my 2017 first date uniform of Calvin Klein undies, jeans so tight they were a second skin and a crisp Fred Perry shirt. I'd leave the flat with levels of confidence usually found in mediocre privately educated straight men but would routinely return home with the disappointment of a misguided X Factor contestant who hadn't made it through to Judges' Houses.

The dating scene was especially brutal for someone who'd recently had their heart broken. After Jane, I was too vulnerable, too intense to really embrace it. And don't make the mistake of imagining that the sapphic scene is any easier than the straight one. Over the years I've had dozens of single hetero gal pals say: 'Ooh, I'd love to be a lesbian, it must be so much easier dating women.' But let me stop you right there. First off, it's a little offensive to ignore the social, economic and misogynist prejudice you experience as an outwardly queer woman, and secondly, lesbian dating is just as confusing and infuriating as dating in the straight world. There are still fuck boys (although they're actually girls), sociopaths, self-obsessives, narcissists, liars, an exceptionally high proportion of women who are still in love with their exes and, occasionally, the line between friendship and relationship can get a little blurred.

In my post-Jane phase, there was one friend I leaned on quite heavily. Because she was also queer, I thought she understood me. We were just friends and she had a girlfriend, but, after a while, we started flirting. I hold my hands up, I loved it. I was a mess and her attention was addictive. She implied that her relationship was on the rocks and that maybe *we* would be better suited than *they* were. I was thrilled. So thrilled, in fact, I drunkenly suggested we give it a go. But the next day, she did the old switcheroo and told her girlfriend that I had confessed feelings for her. I got involved in some real dyke drama, which is like regular drama but everyone is wearing skinny jeans and Doc Martens. She told me she wasn't at all attracted to me, that she would never want to sleep with me, that I must be a narcissist and that she was embarrassed that I had mistaken friendship for flirting. Which, of course, is something I unpacked in therapy for the following twelve months. She did it all on speakerphone so her girlfriend could hear. I imagined them laughing after. I thought my self-worth couldn't be any lower but as she put down the phone I found a surprise basement.

Maybe she was right. Maybe I was so desperate for an attractive woman to spend time with me that I imagined chemistry that was never there, that every friendly word I mistook for a flirtation was a fanciful flight of my bruised little heart. Maybe every look I deemed seductive and suggestive was just an eye complaint I didn't know she had. Or maybe she was just a bit of a c*nt. I guess we will never know.

I am not even sure what that elusive chemistry is. Why do some people give us butterflies, make us fumble our words or smile just by looking at us? I don't understand the biology at all. But after my bad break-up, I was on the hunt for it: chemistry, love and a little bit of the magic Nan and Gramps had found all those years ago.

Finding it for myself was made even more complicated by a seldom-discussed risk when it comes to queer dating – inadvertently being the subject of someone's little experiment.

Don't get me wrong, we all have to start somewhere but there's something strange about going on a date and everything it involves – the nerves, the excitement, that feeling of *what if she's the one* – and not realizing until it's too late that you're merely an exercise in exploring the other person's sexuality. And this happened to me a surprising number of times. One friend reckons it's because

I'm not too girly but also not too boyish. Think of me as the gateway drug before you get to the hard stuff of butches and lipstick femmes.

One night, I arrived at a cool Hackney bar, the sort of place where you can get a mediocre roast on a Sunday for the bargain price of £25. She was sitting on a stool at the bar and she looked nervous. I joined her and before my drink had even arrived, she blurted out: 'I haven't done this before, been on a date with a woman. I didn't want to tell you on the app in case you cancelled, I'm not usually attracted to women but I think maybe I could be.'

Her words and her uncertainty hung in the air as I realized that carefully ironing my shirt had been a wasted errand. I was looking for love and she was trying to *make* herself fancy a woman, any woman. My heart sank a little. I realized this wasn't the night that my epic love story would begin. The fact that I, a woman, was stood in front of her, exfoliated head to toe, and looking as good as it was possible for me to look and she could only muster a weak 'I think maybe' was a low moment for my already wilted self-esteem.

Still, we ended up spending the evening chatting, quickly aware that this wasn't a real date and that we'd probably never see each other again. We were therefore able to speak with the openness usually reserved for very best friends. We drank a lot of wine and spilt our guts. She explained she'd been fucked around by men so much that she thought she'd try being gay for a bit. I explained that it's usually not really something you have a go at like rock climbing or pottery and if you feel like you have to *try* it's probably not for you. I took her through my break-up in violent, technicolour detail. I told her how frightened I was that I would never feel love again, about the friend who was flirty then cruel and that I was lonely even when surrounded by mates. She told me about her parents' messy divorce and her fear that history would repeat itself. Since her teens she'd been in and out of relationships with men. She had inadvertently become 'the one before the one' – a guy would dump her because he wasn't ready for anything serious only to end up engaged 'to some blonde bitch that looks like a model' (her words) a few months later. This had happened three times and had left my temporary best friend shattered and hopeless. After a couple more drinks she agreed that she probably wasn't gay or bi or pan, she was just quite sad and sick of men. I told her it wasn't all men; just the bad ones, that there were thousands of good, kind men out there who would be incredibly lucky to have her. Look at me, standing up for straight dudes. #ally. She reassured me about finding love and told me my ex was a dick for letting 'a catch' (her words again) like me go. We got a lot off our chests, then laughed at the absurdity of our night. Last orders rolled around remarkably quickly. We stepped out into the rough hubbub of a Hoxton night, both a little lighter. As the cool night air hit our faces we also realized we were a little drunk. We hugged and left in opposite directions. I walked back to my flat along the canal in the dark, which in retrospect feels unsafe but I didn't care. For the first time in months I felt like me.

Josh was right, I had reached the moment when I stopped feeling entirely sad. She and I never saw each other again.

We did recently follow one another on Instagram though. Turns out she moved to Australia, got married (to a really fit guy) and became very good at surfing. Good for her. Sometimes, you actually don't need the pressure of a date; instead, a kind stranger, a lack of inhibitions and two bottles of wine can be exactly what you need.

Dating is different for everyone. There are stereotypes that lesbians move in on the second date, gay men find it impossible to settle down, and straight women are desperate to get engaged and forced to wait (im)patiently for their boyfriend to pop the question while dropping hints and crying in the bathroom at other people's weddings. Clearly, stereotypes exist for a reason but I've also known the exact opposite of all these scenarios.

And for queer women, another potential barrier to finding love is not having many options when it comes to meeting one another in real life. My gay male friends, on the other hand, have a plethora of places to visit when they're single and ready to mingle. According to LGBTQIA+ media outlet PinkNews, as of October 2023 there were just three permanent lesbian bars or clubs in the UK, compared to two hundred and twenty-six gay bars. I'm aware that women and non-binary folk are welcome at most of these, but not having our own spaces does make it harder to meet.

And if you're a lesbian with a gay BFF you might occasionally find yourself in spaces that aren't suited to your taste, for example once Tom Allen and I accidently strolled into a dark room in a night club in Vauxhall. A dark room is a room with minimal lighting, where men can be amorous with other men while a very supportive audience watches. 'No Love, this room isn't for you' said a very handsome muscly man in a very small jockstrap as he ushered me gently out of the room. How we laughed.

The closest I've come to this sort of hedonism was being invited to a sex party by a burlesque dancer from Paris, who was wearing a leather policeman's uniform. It was the same weekend as my nan's ninetieth birthday and it didn't feel right to do both in a forty-eight-hour period. Disappointingly a Victoria sponge, a glass of Cinzano and a game of cards in an old people's block is far more my vibe.

So how does someone sick of apps, tired of organizing dates that go nowhere and without anywhere obvious to meet fellow gay women find love? As the months went by, I carried on searching for the One, although, increasingly, I wasn't sure I still believed in the concept, despite the example of my grandparents. The idea of a soulmate, just one person in the world that you're perfect with, started to feel like too much pressure. There are 7.8 billion of us. What are the odds that the one with whom you can reach dizzying heights of love and happiness happens to go to your gym?

Am I starting to sound like less of an old romantic?

I started thinking about how the idea of the One makes you hunt for perfection, and I wasn't even sure what perfection was meant to look like. I certainly didn't feel like *I* was anyone's idea of perfect. I wondered whether my desire for the One – for finding that person who I'd match so completely with – was making me take fewer risks when it came to dating. If you're holding out for someone who has the same interests, likes and dislikes, who prefers a Pizza Hut to a Pizza Express, who wants the exact same thing you do, all of the time, you might end up waiting your whole life. Maybe it was time to remove the One from the equation, to consider someone who *wasn't* just like me. It wouldn't mean I'd have to change myself, as I had done with Jane, I began to realize. Perhaps I needed someone who would open my eyes to new things, someone I'd find *new* hobbies and interests with, but equally, someone I could be apart from. Someone who wasn't my other half but a full person with their own separate life that I'd adore.

And that's exactly what I eventually ended up finding.

I was living with Jenny, a fellow comedian and one of my best friends. She moved in shortly after Jane moved out. She was also newly single and while there was a spare room with all her stuff in it, most nights we shared a bed. We were both in our early thirties but somehow it felt like a teenage sleepover every night, regularly getting the giggles and laughing until one of us would nearly wet ourselves or hyperventilate. Both searching for love we would each go out on dates and realize we preferred to be at home together under a duvet watching *Pitch Perfect*, eating a tub of ice cream and drinking a glass of red. Jenny is straight (much to her disappointment, I assume) but people always thought we were a couple (much to her delight, I assume). And that's what Alice thought too, when we arrived at a wedding together, the wedding where Alice and I were being set up by our mutual friend, the bride, Camille.

A wedding is officially one of the top five most romantic

places to meet your future spouse. The others are Disneyland Paris, the Orient Express, a village pub on Christmas Eve (very Cameron and Jude, another excellent film featuring Kate) and the start line at the London Marathon. I don't make the rules, don't @ me.

I didn't make the best first impression, as Alice thought I had brought a date to a wedding where I knew I was being set up, a dick move by anyone's standards. When Camille first mentioned I might like her friend, I bristled a little: just because we're both single and gay doesn't mean we'll fall for each other, right? But within twenty minutes of chatting to Alice, I could see exactly why Camille thought we'd get on. She was interesting, chatty, she made me laugh, she was beautiful and she had a gentle confidence that I found incredibly sexy. We even discussed politics early on. It's not a particularly hot subject but important to get your allegiance out in the open at the start. I may have been, by then, up for meeting someone different from me, but opposing moral views is a bit of a deal-breaker. We locked eyes as we talked. I finally felt that elusive thing: chemistry. I didn't want our conversation to end. The cacophony of the wedding hummed into background noise and all I could focus on was her eyes and our mutual feelings on the UK's embarrassing political landscape. A brass band started and we were all encouraged/instructed/commanded to get on the dance floor for a brassy rendition of Beyoncé's 'Love on Top', which was absolutely banging to be fair. We went and danced with our respective friends but spent the night sharing flirty glances across the room. We made a vague plan to meet for a 'drink some time'.

Less than twelve hours later I slid into her DMs. Turned out 'some time' was later that same week.

I was excited but also a little apprehensive. What if the spark I felt at the wedding was just the booze and that hopeful joy that comes over you when you watch two loved-up friends say: 'I do'? I started getting ready ridiculously early, I changed three times. In the end I opted for a checked jacket and my trademark skinny jeans. We went to a cocktail bar near my house. I felt at ease with Alice almost at once. She makes everyone feel comfortable. She later told me she was 'utterly shitting it' but it didn't show. We started chatting and didn't stop for three hours, or rather two espresso martinis, a bottle of wine, a whisky for her and an amaretto for me. It was clear from the start that in lots of ways we were quite different. She works in the City, doing a proper job, the type where she has to go to big important meetings wearing a formal dress. She does presentations, discusses data and numbers (are they the same thing?), company culture and responsible investments. She knows exactly who she is, and has a group of brilliant friends (always an excellent sign). She told me she volunteered as a 'big sister' at a charity for children in the care system which revealed so much about her. She has terrible taste in music – she loves really loud, bang-bang clubbing tunes, but hey, no one is completely perfect. There was a directness to her that I found both intimidating and refreshing. The book in her bag, a historical fiction, was intimidatingly thick, too, but most importantly she made me feel seen and she made me laugh, more than most stand-ups.

At 10 p.m. I had to leave to check on my cat, Velma, who had been spayed earlier that day. (Oh, the sexy romance! Just so you know I do appreciate what a lesbian cliché I am.) Alice said she'd walk me back. Sod it, she'd come up for a drink. We stopped in a Tesco for a bottle of red. While reading the labels and pretending I knew more about grapes than I did, she leaned in to kiss me. 'No, our first kiss can't be in a Tesco Express on the Kingsland Road,' I whispered. I knew, I knew immediately in fact, that this was a first kiss I would need to tell my friends about. It couldn't happen next to a sign for half-price Paprika Pringles with a Clubcard.

The thing I was most in awe of was how much Alice had her shit together. She was still only in her late twenties and she was more at home in herself than most forty-year-olds I know. I'd been looking for a soulmate who was just like me, but on the surface, and to the untrained eye, Alice and I couldn't have been more different. She was organized, not anxious, not even a little bit highly strung. But it was underneath all that that our similarities shone: our morals, ambition, hopes and values were perfectly in sync. I'd thought that relationships should be all-consuming, like Romeo and Juliet – although they were teenagers who both ended up dead because of a misunderstanding with a friar so I'm not sure their relationship should be an inspiration. Alice was calm and collected. She had a busy life and so did I but we were delighted to make time for each other.

To begin with I was scared. Scared to let her in. Scared

that this brilliant woman would be added to a list of people it didn't work out with, and 20 per cent of me wanted to run away: what was the point? It was bound to end in heartbreak yet again. But the other 80 per cent wanted to move in together next week. That bloody stereotype.

Alice and I quickly became a couple and for the first time in my entire life I felt at ease. I didn't feel like I had to prove anything to her. I just trusted that she liked spending time with me. My best friends loved her: they thought I had hit the jackpot. Jenny said one night as we lay in bed watching the Barden Bellas singing at the a cappella championships yet again: 'You've found her, Suz, she's the one you've been looking for.' After knowing Alice for only a couple of months, I knew she wasn't the type to lie to me or be careless with my feelings. She wouldn't bother wasting her time. She didn't need me. So many previous relationships, in retrospect, felt transactional in one way or another. I didn't need her either. We just wanted each other. More than anything else.

I was honest with Alice, in ways I hadn't been before, or with anyone (well, until I started writing this book). I find the world overwhelming a lot of the time. For so long I found that embarrassing to admit. I am often busy, flustered, sometimes I have to sit still because my brain feels like it needs to be anchored and chances are I haven't organized things to make my life easier. In fact, I am usually running late because I've lost track of time and started reading an article on my bed while wrapped in a towel. Often, it's not even a good article. Then I will remember three friends I have forgotten to reply to and decide they simply must be responded to at that very moment. I am always running late for a train that I haven't bought a ticket for. And I mean that in both the literal and the metaphorical senses. Alice, on the other hand, has always bought her ticket weeks ago. Frankly, she may as well be driving the train. She'd have time to grab a coffee, pet a dog and chat with any neighbour she meets on the way. She has a calm and a tranquil energy that makes everything less overwhelming for me.

But don't confuse that relaxed energy for her being a Debbie Downer – she's also fun and spontaneous. For example, a month in, she took me on a date to Paris. A pretty baller move, we can all agree. We got the Eurostar to Gare du Nord, had an excellent meal and stayed in a really cute hotel. The following day we went to Disneyland Paris – she had remembered that at the wedding I had drunkenly mentioned wanting to go and see Mickey and the gang but exes in the past thought it was a childish waste of holiday time. (What was I doing with my life?) She found three empty days in my diary, told me to keep them free and took me. To make it even better, when we got there Jenny and her new boyfriend, Dan, were waiting to surprise me outside Sleeping Beauty's castle. We spent the day in Mickey ears behaving like children. We rode the Hyperspace Mountain four times and then all felt pretty rough for the next hour. It remains one of my favourite days ever. As I said, a pretty baller move.

One night, when we'd been together for a few months, we were at the house of one of my friends and it was full of comedians. We were laughing and joking, the comics all teasing each other (a real sign of affection in my friendship group). I made fun of Alice. In my mind I was trying to include her but the look on her face told me that not only had I isolated her but I'd offended her too. Her look told me everything and I quickly changed the subject. Later, when we were walking home in the smallest hours of the morning, Alice stopped and calmly told me: 'I don't want to be in a relationship where we take shots at each other, even if it's just for a joke. That might be cool with your friends, but it's not with me.' I instantly loved her even more. I didn't want to be in a relationship where we belittled or took the piss out of each other either, even if it was just for a laugh. It felt petty and juvenile. I learnt a great lesson that night.

She taught me the most important thing in a relationship is kindness. I didn't feel like I needed to be something I wasn't or constantly prove myself. I wasn't on tenterhooks waiting for something to go wrong. This had a huge impact on my anxiety. I trusted I had someone in my corner, that if everything went tits up she'd still love me. Her love made me like myself. I thought: if this wonderful person wants to spend their time with me, I guess I must be pretty good too. My self-worth had never been so high which meant my anxiety had no choice but to shrink.

I realized love isn't something that needs huge public displays of affection, to be shouted from a rooftop, or expensive presents, or some big essay on Instagram about how they are your 'light in the dark'. (Which as a side note I do find very strange. Surely if it's your partner's birthday it's easier to just lean across the bed and tell them you love them rather than taking the time to post some mushy *Guardian*-long read under the fittest picture you can find of them, probably from when you first met so you're both looking a bit hotter and a bit younger.) Love is actually a partnership. It's knowing that you have a co-pilot no matter what. It's someone holding your hand through the rough and the smooth. Alice told me I was enough just as I was, reminding me of Mark Darcy in the best possible way.

Maybe it wasn't Nan and Gramps's war-torn love story, but I quickly learnt that being next to her made every part of my life better.

OK, vom, enough. This isn't a romance novel but I did want to write about love because, as you'll know from previous chapters, it's something that, for a long time, I didn't think I would have. It was something I felt I didn't deserve. But Alice taught me I did.

I wouldn't call her my soulmate because I'm not really sure that exists but she is my best friend and my mate for life. I believe that knowing I have her has changed part of my brain and all of my soul, but I don't know quite how.

．　．　．

So I am going to talk to therapist and *Married at First Sight*'s sex and relationship expert Charlene Douglas about how we can love fully after being hurt and what can we do to help us not only find enduring love but also, to keep it.

Charlene and first I met a few years ago, on a TV spin-off show about *Married at First Sight*. I warmed to her immediately. She's frank, but hugely compassionate and insightful when it comes to all matters of the heart. The first question I ask her is what actually happens in our bodies and brains when we fall in love.

'The excited feelings we experience when we fall in love can make our heartbeat race, give us "butterflies" in our bellies and can lead us to daydream as we constantly think about our loved one. We might trip over our words when we're in their presence or notice that as a result of the release of pleasure-related hormones like dopamine, oxytocin and serotonin our bodies feel tingly and excited. It's an adrenaline rush – it makes you feel excited, euphoric, sometimes unable to sleep and eat. It's really quite exciting.

'This chemistry might be referred to as the elusive "honeymoon" period, a time when you see your new partner through rose-tinted lenses, when the excitement and the newness of the relationship just seems to envelop you.'

I think a lot of us know that feeling, that buzz, even if it's just a crush. The right amount of dopamine and other hormones can make you feel alert, motivated, happy and craving more.

'That's right,' says Charlene. 'The point at which you're engaged in a pleasurable act with a partner is when dopamine is released. It gives us the "I want more" effect and triggers the effects of arousal.'

So how do we keep that attraction and chemistry going long-term?

'Well,' Charlene shrugs. 'In reality, that might not be what you want. Although these feelings can feel amazing, usually during this height of euphoria the frontal cortex (the part of our brain that enables us to make rational and sensible decisions) shuts off. So you're far more likely to ignore red flags during this period. This is why we may find that once we are out of the "honeymoon phase" (usually the first few months of falling for a partner), we might see behaviours from them that we didn't realize were an issue before.

I guess that's when we have to start understanding the different feelings between love and lust. I wondered what the actual differences are between the two states.

'Lust,' Charlene tells me, 'is more of a temporary state of overwhelming sexual attraction. But love involves a deeper, more emotional connection (that may or may not include sex). You may feel more able to be your true self, and you have a genuine care for the other person. Love allows you to care for and consider the other person, whereas lust is usually all about your own sexual desires. It's less about keeping that elusive honeymoon period alive, and more about combining that new relationship excitement with some of our more rational thinking.'

Alice and I have been together for nearly eight years and I think she would be comfortable with me telling you that our relationship doesn't have that brand-new excitement any more. It still has excitement, don't get me wrong, but not in that all-consuming, obsessive way it did in the first couple of years. Mainly because that would be exhausting. So how can we keep the spark alive in a marriage or a long-term relationship?

'The key to that is to make sure that you regularly check in with each other. Now, I know the idea of a date night can feel quite dated, but it's so important because you need to be able to come back together, have fun, be playful with each other, and kind of review your relationship. I know that sounds really serious, but I think it's important to keep the spark alive.'

Reviewing your relationship does sound like you're going to give it a star rating and print it in a broadsheet but, in some ways, Alice and I have been doing a version of that – a sort of relationship check-in – since we started living together. We didn't call it that but we would find time, often over a glass of wine or a Sunday brunch, to make sure the other was feeling good about our relationship, if there were any ways either one of us needed more support with something in particular, to make sure we were on the same page about our hopes and desires. It became even more important when we began thinking about parenting – how we would parent as a team and where we would like to live to do that. And in the beginning it *did* feel quite serious but it means that now we find potentially tough conversations easier. In fact, I'd say it's helped us to fall in love with each other more as we change and grow.

Charlene notes: 'In a good relationship, I agree those check-ins happen naturally. The way that life works is that, usually, unless you're super lucky, it throws some kind of curveball your way. And that then gives your relationship an opportunity to demonstrate its strength.'

We definitely felt that during our journey to parenthood and when we became mums.

Talking to Charlene, I realized our 'relationship check-ins' early on were probably vital to its survival while I was still delicate. When I turned up at that wedding in September 2017 I was bruised. I was anxious (what a surprise) about letting someone in. I was OK with going out on dates – despite not really enjoying them – but when deeper feelings began to surface, it felt like a real leap to allow myself to fall in love again, now that I knew the dangers of heartbreak. I asked Charlene for her advice on how we should go all in again, without fear.

'I think that it's impossible to walk into a new relationship when you've been hurt before without having an element of anxiety. But what you need to look for is evidence that you can feel emotionally safe with someone. Then you will get to a point where you start to relax and get back to what we said about hormones. That oxytocin – the love-bonding hormone – kicks in where you feel safe and you feel relaxed. Obviously, I'm a sex therapist, so I always bring it back to sex. You will have the best sex ever because good sex is about being safe with someone.'

Finding safety in a relationship doesn't sound particularly romantic or sexy but it's those foundational building blocks that all the fun stuff can sit on. Like a house: yes, the high ceilings, huge windows and exposed beams are the beauty but you don't get any of that without a load-bearing structure below it. (Yes, I've just googled 'How do you build a house?')

I've always believed that having my heart broken made me a better partner to Alice. I asked Charlene whether she thought that a little bit of heartbreak can be a positive for your next relationship.

'I do,' she says. 'I think it grounds you. In the moment it's the worst thing ever, right? Every sad song that you ever sang in your teen years now makes sense. Sinéad O'Connor singing with that one tear. It now makes sense. And from a therapist point of view, we liken it to grief. Over time, though, break-ups allow you the space to look at what you really want from a relationship, and what your values are. They help you decide what's important to you, and what's not.'

Finally, I wanted to ask Charlene for advice for others who might be trying to meet someone. Before I met Alice, I was so sick of the apps, and of how hard it was to find a real connection.

'There are two things that come to my mind here. One is your own personal well-being, looking after yourself, making sure your life is full and happy and that you've got the friendships, that you have got a good social life, that you're excited about life. I know it's the classic therapist line but when you're in that really good space, you gravitate towards other people that have good energy as well. And next, I'd say when you speak to a lot of single people, they spend a lot of time in spaces where they aren't going to meet people that they are going to fancy. I think the older you get, you're probably not going out as much, or you're just going to your parents' house, or your friend's house, or just going down to the bar or the pub. So you do have to be a bit more strategic in terms of spaces that you are in to meet somebody.'

Timing is everything when it comes to relationships. You could meet an awesome person but just not be in the right space for it in your life. So finding peace within yourself is a massive part of being ready to find that relationship. I was really interested in what Charlene said about where you might meet a future partner. As you know, I met Alice at a wedding but I was interested in where some of my friends met their loves. Here are the answers I got:

Introduced by a friend

A language class

At Glastonbury Festival

Working together

Studying together

A fitness class

A book club

A community choir

And, of course, Grindr (lol)

Looking for love and falling in love makes you enormously vulnerable. In my opinion it's an act of bravery to really go for it all guns blazing, but it's also about feeling full and contented in other areas of your life too. To quote the great RuPaul: 'If you can't love yourself, how the hell you gonna love somebody else?'

CHAPTER 7

Is becoming someone's wife fundamentally anti-feminist?

Forty-two per cent of marriages end in divorce. Sorry to be such a mood hoover at the top of the chapter, especially when I have just whanged on about falling in love. But that's the truth, baby!

Last year there were 131,000 weddings in the UK. That's a lot of flowers, but the likelihood is that more than 55,020 of those couples will end up divorced. The cost of the average wedding in the UK at the time of writing this is £30,000, which is a lot of money for something that only works out 58 per cent of the time. But rather than find that statistic depressing, I think it's sweet – life-affirming – that so many people still choose to get married, knowing the odds aren't great. Believing their love will survive. Sweet but possibly stupid. And in 2021 I became one of those idiots.

Marrying Alice is easily the best thing I have ever done, and I have swum with dolphins, met two Spice Girls and played the Royal Albert Hall (ten minutes on a charity show but it totally counts). Knowing that Alice and I face life together makes my world a much better place. I know I always have someone on my team, that we always root for one another and put each other first. I love having a wife, I love being a wife, I love calling Alice my wife. The word 'partner' is fine but it does sometimes sound like we are either high-powered lawyers who own a firm together, or cowboys. And although I love the aesthetic of both, we are neither.

There isn't an expectation around who should propose in a same-sex relationship, which I think makes it more exciting. It's like playing Buckaroo: it could happen at any time. Some straight women I know have moaned for years about their boyfriend's inability to buy a ring. When I have suggested they pop the question themselves they look at me like I'm on crack, like that would be the most ludicrous and desperate thing imaginable. Even though they *are* desperate, absolutely desperate, to get down that aisle but heaven forbid they take action to make it happen. I have never understood this; if you really love someone, why wouldn't you tell them that you'd love to marry them? I wonder if they fear emasculating their partners or worry that suggesting lifelong commitment might make them run for the hills. I would say that if you truly suspect your partner would react in either of those ways, you should be the one warming up and getting your trainers on.

Alice proposed to me, and I knew it was going to happen. Let me be clear: I am not a psychic. I didn't get a feeling and just *know*. My mum let slip. That's right, my mum ruined my proposal. Although her intentions were good, it did somewhat botch Alice's big plans. Around eighteen months into our relationship, it was pretty clear to us both that we wanted to make a go of this for life. (We probably knew that after date two tbh.) (Nothing like leaning into those stereotypes, is there?) Alice asked my mum for her permission, which I thought was very sweet but a real f**k-you to my very alive and present father. A few weeks later Mum and I went out for a drink and Mum said in no uncertain terms that if I thought Alice was the one (she made it very clear that *she* did) I should get her a ring to 'always have in your back pocket . . . wink wink nudge nudge'. She actually said 'wink wink nudge nudge'. So I did.

I knew Alice had made the decision to pop the question and while I didn't want to beat her to it, I did like the idea of having a ring to give her too. I knew Alice would have organized something classy, understated but brilliant. About a month later, we were packing to go away for the weekend and she seemed nervous, jittery even. It turned out that she had planned to pop the question when we were drinking cocktails at a fancy country hotel, looking out on to beautiful countryside at sunset, but the tension got to her and she blurted out: 'I love you and I think we should get married,' then opened a box containing my perfect version of an engagement ring, vintage art deco. Immediately, I said yes, then ran to my knicker drawer and pulled out the diamond that I had hidden weeks before. And there, in our pokey flat in Hoxton that had mould on the wall, was too hot in the summer and too cold in the winter, we decided to try for ever. Shortly after we both said yes the cat had a piss in the litter box, then scratched around in it for what felt like an eternity. Classy, understated, brilliant.

On Instagram, I posted the classic back-of-the-hand ring pic with a smiley, surprised face (you know the one). I did this mainly to cut out the admin of texting everyone; it's the modern-day equivalent of a marriage announcement in the newspaper. Alongside the congratulatory messages from our friends, I received a direct message from a stranger: 'That isn't very feminist!' What could be more feminist, I thought, than marrying another woman? I got a number of messages like that, both about feminism, and questioning my need, as a gay woman, to commit to the heteronormative status quo. Was one of us going to change our name? Why did I feel the need to do something so outdated?

The comments made me look back and try to remember my first feminist act. I've always been opinionated and unafraid to show my feelings, and my mum will confirm that that was my vibe straight out of the womb, but my first proper feminist undertaking was arguing with my PE teacher in Year 9. Not that I would have known the word – we didn't learn about feminism at school and it wasn't discussed around my kitchen table. It was Portsmouth in the early noughties, we'd only just got a desktop computer. But now, I can see my row with Mrs P (not the one with fifteen pockets) for what it was. We had PE twice a week and while many of the girls would feign 'women's troubles' to get out of their PE kit, I couldn't wait to get into mine. I don't want to brag but I am naturally sporty. Swimmer's shoulders, I was told, making me confident in the pool and insecure in strappy tops. While I found many lessons at school a trial, due to my dyslexia and probable ADHD, in PE I thrived. When you're made to feel like a bit of a dunce in the rest of the classes, having one where you come out on top wasn't just satisfying, it was vital. There in my PE kit, with the scabs on my knees from my inexperience with a razor, I was told that in the first part of the term the boys would play football and the girls netball.

'What?' So many of the girls are apparently on their period we barely have a team! 'I want to play football,' I begged, because netball was rubbish (sorry to any netball enthusiasts). I didn't want to wear a bib and pivot, I didn't want to wear one of those short, pleated skirts with big cotton granny pants underneath. I wanted to get deep in a tackle (for once in my life). Mrs P wouldn't have it and none of the other girls seemed to care: they were far more interested in not getting sweaty and flirting with the Year 11 boys. I pleaded: 'Football is so much more fun and dramatic, *please* let me play. I don't mind playing with the boys, anything but netball!' Mrs P mocked: 'You can't play with the boys, you wouldn't keep up.' I saw red.

I was told if I wanted to do PE at all this term I had to play netball because I was a girl. This set off some sort of volcano in my head. The heat rose, my hands clenched, fury spilt out. *Why? Why couldn't I play football? What difference would it really make? Why did the boys always get an unfair advantage with everything? Why were we treated so differently?* I was livid, apoplectic at how unjust it felt. I chucked my bib on the floor, stormed off like a petulant toddler and was promptly given detention for my actions. It was 'unladylike', my head of year told me. I was a hormonal, closeted teenager in a rage, as if I gave two hoots about being ladylike. What was worse was that I had seen boys express themselves through anger several times – one threw a chair at the teacher – and while they were reprimanded, it was considered that boys were allowed to show anger. It seemed that their behaviour was tolerated, expected even; that when they had fights or shouted or pinged our bra straps it was just boys being boys. It was so unfair. While I have always been very at home in my gender I remember wishing that I was a boy because it was clear from my teenage perspective that they had a much easier life. I just wanted to be treated the same as them, to have the same opportunities. I just wanted to kick a bloody football for half a term.

'Feminist' was a dirty word when I was a teen. It was also coded language for a lesbian, therefore you can imagine how much I didn't want to be called one. So I joined in when people mocked feminists as man-hating, bra-burning, head cases. I remember a young adult at after-school club telling me that 'feminists don't want equality, they want revenge. They don't need men at all. They want to get rid of all the men in power and run everything.' Outwardly, I tutted and shook my head in agreement. Obviously inside I thought this was a great idea and one I could fully get behind.

I am ashamed to say that I was in my early twenties before I was happy to describe myself as a feminist. But once I'd come out as a lesbian, it became a lot easier to add feminist too, and I soon became equally proud to be both. So I did question whether I was letting the side down by getting hitched. While I try not to listen to what strangers on the internet say (if I did I would be lost in a constant, hourly cycle of fluctuating between being an ego-mad bighead and giving up comedy entirely) it bothered me in the background as we started planning our wedding.

While wandering around beautiful venues I wondered why I felt the need to make this big display? Was it something to do with telling the world I was lovable? Possibly. Was part of it a f**k-you to people who said we couldn't or we shouldn't? Almost certainly.

After all, it was only ten years ago that marriage was even made legal for your best lezzie pal Suz. When I first came out I never thought it would be possible for me to get married. At the time I said I didn't care: 'Why would I want to have some boring old-fashioned marriage?' But this was a lie. Of course I wanted the same rights and celebrations as my straight mates and not being granted them ate away at my self-worth. Knowing that the government, the Church and plenty of people felt my relationship would never be worthy enough for marriage – that mattered. Knowing that, to some, my love would always be lesser, less real, less important, less valid, had a real effect on me. The Civil Partnership Act allowed a marriage of sorts, but it felt unfair to many within the LGBTQIA+ community. A civil partnership seemed to be more about the legalities of marriage than the beautiful, joyful celebration. You signed a civil document rather than entering vows which feels rather grey by comparison. Civil partnerships were made law back in 2005, but it passed me by. I was in my second year of drama school, desperately hoping my boyfriend would magically turn me straight.

But thirteen years later, when I actually got engaged, I was out and coming closer to being proud. Indeed, I'd been one of tens of thousands of people who'd marched to Parliament Square in support of equal marriage but as I stamped my Doc Martens up Whitehall I couldn't help but wonder (who am I, Carrie Bradshaw?) whether it was archaic that I even wanted to engage in something which, as those Instagram detractors went on to point out, is traditionally about the ownership of women? Something that is traditionally about a man literally giving his daughter to another man under the watchful eye of (checks notes) another man in a dog collar, to love, honour and obey. Surely that doesn't sit right for most women in the present day.

And is it different for gays and theys? Should I just reject the whole thing entirely? I know that some people within the queer community feel that marriage is selling out. For some, it's seen as apeing a straight relationship – a bride in a dress, a bride in a suit, like playing at husband and wife, when part of being queer is stepping outside of the norm and being comfortably punk in otherness. Should I put my foot down and say: no, I will not partake in this bizarre ancient ritual, steeped in misogyny, in front of a God I'm not sure I believe in? But then again, declaring your desire to spend for ever together in front of your family and friends, toasting to love, putting on your Sunday best and doing 'Oops Upside Your Head' with all your aunties and uncles is a good day out.

Is becoming someone's wife fundamentally anti-feminist?

It's obviously more than that. In spite of marriage's problematic history, it's still ever so popular. To us, tying the knot felt like the epitome of togetherness and security. And why shouldn't a same-sex couple have access to that? We shouldn't feel that we have to fall in line with the heterosexual life model but if what I wanted was a marriage – a marriage like my parents have, like the one my grandparents, Jack and Joan, had – then surely proper feminism, and proper LGBTQIA+ rights, is letting me have that choice. And I love being married. Obviously that has a lot to do with who I have chosen to marry. I know people that have married real planks and honestly *that* looks like an absolute ball ache.

Originally, marriage had almost nothing to do with love and attraction. As little as a hundred years ago mutual desire wasn't considered important – marriage was about forming alliances, expanding the family labour force, and inheritance of land and status. Alice brought precisely zero land to our marriage but I do think she's improved my status.

We set a date for the following year: May 2020. Perfect! We booked Hoxton Hall, just down the road from the flat. It's a gorgeous little music hall because if there's an opportunity to get onstage, let's face it, I'll take it. We planned the food and music, we persuaded some of our talented pals to sing and play instruments. I booked a tailor. Alice found a very cool, slightly Gothic black dress. We decided some parts of the traditional marriage ritual weren't for us. We didn't want any religion, any obeying, and we certainly weren't being 'given away'. Some things we loved though: exchanging of rings, promising to love one another through the ups and downs of life and saying 'I do'. We wanted the vows. A humanist service sounded just right for us. We had planning meetings and paid deposits. We invited 180 people. We'd agreed on 150 but I kept bumping into comedians at gigs and inviting them along. We figured the more the merrier. It was going to be a great day! What could possibly go wrong?

Eastenders duff duffs*

We didn't cancel until April 2020. For the first couple of weeks of lockdown, we genuinely thought all this Covid business would be over by May. How little we knew. We kept trying to rebook the wedding, finding new dates that were then postponed, over and over again. Each time, it was gutting. When our wedding got snatched from our finger-tips, I realized how much I wanted it. Yes to the big piss-up, the dancing, the public displays of love (which usually I find a bit much but at a wedding, totally acceptable), but more than that I just wanted to be married to Alice. I wanted it recorded that we are family. I wanted our lives to be inex-tricably linked in the history books so scholars of the future could trace our shared existence. I wanted our great-great granddaughter to be able to get a hefty book off a library shelf and see our names next to each other in timeworn ink.

But Covid put the idea of marriage to bed. We decided we'd do it when we could, but the constant booking and cancelling was killing our vibe. Although we still mentioned our nuptials regularly, they were more of a lockdown fantasy like learning a language or writing a novel than anything else. Our life continued. Our daughter arrived. We became a family of three.

More than a year after our cancelled wedding, we popped to the multistorey Sainsbury's one afternoon, because we know how to have a good time. It was still deep enough into the pandemic that a wander around the homeware section felt like a European city break. I pushed the buggy as Alice loaded up the trolley with unfamiliar groceries in a desperate attempt to make mealtimes as exciting as possible. We got some new bedding as a treat, from Holly Willoughby's home range. I don't know where she finds the time. I was reaching for a couple of Gü pots (salted caramel millionaire's shortbread) when Alice said: 'I think we should get married.' I briefly worried she'd been concussed while I was choosing bananas. Yes, dear, I thought, we agreed on doing that a few years ago. But she went on: she was sick of waiting, she wanted to be wives, however the wedding ended up looking. I agreed. I felt the exact same.

Moments later I nipped outside and rang Bromley town hall. I asked when they had the next available slot for a marriage. It was next Wednesday at 9.20. We'd take it! And just a week later Alice and I stood, masked up, in front of a registrar, with our best friends Ruth and Alina, and said 'I do' in a fifteen-minute ceremony while our friend Ross and our little daughter played in the park just outside the building. Our wedding photos are us in front of a vaccine poster next to Bromley town hall car park. Classy, hilarious and a real snapshot in time. We headed back to ours where Tom was waiting with champagne and had a literal wedding breakfast (yes, we were all allowed inside together at this point). It wasn't the wedding I had imagined. For starters it was in the kitchen-come-living room of a two-bed flat in Sydenham. There was a lot more baby food and a lot less dancing. I hadn't imagined I would have to stop eating halfway through a pancake to go and change someone's nappy but it was perfect. Just seven of us, laughing, in a room full of love.

It was official, we were married. 'Wived' if you will, and while we loved each other just as much as we had the day before there was a difference, a slight shift that we both noted, like clicking in the final Lego piece of one of the architect masters sets.

．　．　．

Has the role of marriage changed in society? Has equal marriage changed marriage for our straight mates too? Why do so many of us still fantasize about walking down the aisle? I am going to talk to activist, writer and founder of the Everyday Sexism Project, Laura Bates, about what marriage means today and whether I have let the sisterhood down.

I first met Laura more than a decade ago, when I did a gig to raise funds for her No More Page Three campaign. We hadn't seen each other for a long time but I have watched her literary success and continued fight for women's rights with appreciation from the sidelines. Being such a vocal activist, I wondered if she experienced the same backlash and internal wrestling when she chose to marry.

'I stupidly wrote an article about getting married, and just got lots of people saying: this is a betrayal, this is outrageous,' she tells me. 'But I think it's more complicated than that. I think it depends on the relationship and on what the marriage is going to be like. I think you can acknowledge that marriage is a historically patriarchal institution and still choose to have an egalitarian marriage. Equally, you can choose to eschew marriage because it's an inherently patriarchal institution but then still have a really unequal relationship'.

And then we got into the statistics and I was here for it.

'Heterosexual relationships are inherently often patriarchal. Women do sixty per cent more housework than men, or seventy minutes more per day. Ninety-one per cent of men climaxed in their last sexual encounter, compared to sixty-four per cent of heterosexual women. So whether or not you get married isn't going to fix those massive inequalities. Those exist across partnerships, whether people are married or not.'

As a gay woman I didn't feel societal or familial pressure to marry but I know some of my straight female friends felt it from both angles.

'There are so many outdated societal pressures and expectations on women that have not progressed with the times,' Laura agrees. 'Pressure to have babies and children, pressure to get married. I think there's still a really dramatic and surprising percentage of our society that thinks that you have to be married to have children. And part of it comes from stories that we grew up with and the extent to which finding a partner (and that partner being heteronormative, being a man), getting married to that partner and then having children is so much of the structure of children's television, children's movies, everything.

Obviously, classics like *Cinderella, Sleeping Beauty, Rapunzel, Snow White*, all of those fairy tales are still a really significant part of kids' childhoods. But you see it even if you look at the more modern, supposedly more egalitarian movies, like *Frozen*, which is absolutely hailed for being this great alternative where it's not the love of a man that saves the heroine and rescues her, it's the love of her sister. But even then, the sequel and a significant plot line is still all about getting engaged.'

Oh man, not Elsa and Anna too!

I really hated the idea of being 'given away' but I know not everyone does. It can be just a nice moment for a father and daughter to share. I ask Laura what she thinks about the tradition.

'For a lot of people, being walked down the aisle or just walking down the aisle with a parent that they love is something that's always been important to them. In their interpretation it's about love for their dad, not because they think he owns them, and I get that. I think we're so obsessed with this idea of "Are you a good or bad feminist?" And I feel like it's bullshit. It's really important that one woman's feminism isn't forced on to another. Surely the point of equality is that we have more agency and the decision-making power to live a life that suits us and makes us happy without throwing our sisters under the bus.

'If you think women and men should be treated equally, you're not the Devil if you want to walk down the aisle with your dad, it's OK. Yes, it has its roots in horrendous, awful, sexist traditions but I think sometimes we put too much importance on these kind of quite arbitrary specific moments rather than the bigger picture.'

I guess it's all about doing it your own way, and finding something that works for you, I suggest.

'Definitely,' says Laura. 'One of the things that's really fun and exciting and positive is how loads of people are finding their own way to totally subvert and change those traditions. So, you've got couples who choose to walk down the aisle together. You've got couples where the groom chooses to walk down the aisle with his parents. There's that sense of families merging, of finding the parts of the tradition that are meaningful to you and discarding the other bits. I know there will be some people who would say: no, by in any way participating in this masquerade with its patriarchal roots, you are inherently perpetuating it and tacitly condoning it. But I think that's too draconian. The problem isn't marriage itself, it's what it represented about wider society.'

Our talk turns to divorce. I ask Laura for her thoughts about why, when divorce rates are higher than ever, tens of thousands of people marry each year in this country alone. Her view on divorce surprised me – it was a lot more positive than how I'd thought of it before.

'I mean, divorce rates being higher is, probably, actually a very positive thing because it means that you're not being trapped. People aren't being trapped with abusers or in completely ridiculously unequal partnerships.'

It's such a great point. Perhaps the fact that the divorce rate is high actually reflects how marriage itself has evolved past its previous, anti-feminist iteration. Today, if someone isn't happy in a marriage they can leave – but before, when a woman was effectively owned, they couldn't. Obviously there are still scenarios where people are trapped in relationships but the rate of divorce does suggest there's more autonomy.

Marriage is still such a new thing for the LGBTQIA+ community and I wondered if the introduction of same-sex marriage might change societal views on heterosexual marriage, too.

'I hope so,' says Laura, 'but I also feel like maybe that's an unfair burden to place on same-sex couples. They've been excluded for so, so long. And then as soon as we finally do make the process equal, we expect them to be the ones to drag marriage into the twenty-first century. That seems really unfair. But I hope it helps people to broaden their minds and to broaden the conceptualization of what marriage can be, moving it away from that very heteronormative, outdated patriarchal assumption about women obeying and submitting.'

You are welcome, world. First we gave you pop music, interior decor and hot pants and now we've fixed marriage. Seriously though, I was heartened to think that the natural equality within a same-sex marriage could be empowering for women in heterosexual relationships.

Alice is very at home with her feminist credentials and she took my name. I believe these things aren't mutually exclusive. She was happy to become a Ruffell. We liked the idea of all sharing a family name, and we suspected, correctly, that it would make life easier for boring household paperwork and for travelling. We didn't want to double-barrel our names – the combination didn't roll off the tongue and it does suggest that in a few generations' time everyone might have six surnames, which feels a lot. Monogramming a towel would take all day.

I was interested in Laura's take on forgoing your family name for your partner's.

'Part of the problem,' she muses, 'is that there isn't a good alternative. It puts people in a really difficult situation, and again, it's the women that end up getting it in the neck.

'It's women that end up being absolutely castigated for not being a good feminist [when they take their male partner's name]. But when society isn't set up in a way that gives you any positive alternatives, you end up being stuck between a rock and a hard place, which feels really unfair. We should be saying: this is a ridiculous system, and trying to find alternatives. Personally,' she adds, 'I do struggle with it. It's not something I would ever do, to take a man's name. And I think that is so obviously bound up in that idea of women's identities being completely obliterated and then being subsumed into just being an extension of the person that they married.

'On the other hand, I think there are examples of people who obviously do it for really positive reasons. I also know people who have chosen a completely new name for themselves and start fresh. But there is no ideal solution yet, because even in that situation you're going to have family members who may feel really sad about the name not carrying on. And I know friends where, in a heterosexual marriage, the man has taken the wife's name. I think that's really lovely. Maybe what we need is for all men in heterosexual relationships to agree that now we've done it this way for however many hundred years, for the next five hundred years, let the men take wives' names in heterosexual marriages, and then we'll reassess.'

Brilliant, that's that sorted then. Make marriage work on your own terms, don't expect other feminists to have the same opinion on everything as you and let's normalize taking the bride's surname. Let's check in 2525. Pop it in your diary, hon.

CHAPTER 8

How do you know you're not f**king up your kids?

As a teenager I assumed the only way I would get to be a parent was if I stayed in the closet and married a man. It confirmed to my teenage brain that being gay was less than; it fed into my adolescent anxiety that the only way I could be happy was if I disregarded every innate intimate impulse, that if I eliminated that part of myself, one day I could fulfil my dream of being a mum.

What I didn't know was that gay folks could and were being parents, that it had been proved time and time again that having same-sex parents has zero negative impact on children, but that wasn't in the general discourse or media. It certainly wasn't celebrated. So the fact that I am a mum, the fact that this dream happened for me, is the greatest part of my life. It is the biggest unexpected joy I could have imagined. (To be clear, my baby wasn't unexpected: having a child in a same-sex relationship is minutely researched, planned and longed for.) She is my joy and she has taught me to love more than I knew was possible. She has enriched my life beyond belief. Not financially, of course – she's an absolute drain.

Not long after we met, I told Alice I saw a child in my future. I wasn't looking into a crystal ball pretending to be Mystic Meg, I just wanted to be honest and frank. 'I really want to be a Mum one day,' I told her. I longed to be one, in fact, but it didn't have to happen soon and I didn't really know how I wanted to do it: IUI, IVF, adoption. I knew I didn't feel the need to have a biological link to my child, or to be the one to carry, I just wanted someone to call me Mum. I wanted to make someone's breakfast; have someone to read bedtime stories to, to bake cakes with. I wanted to teach a little someone how to ride a bike and be the person to pick them up and kiss them better when they fell. So, a few years into our relationship, we started attending seminars in private fertility hospitals and presentation evenings in community centres to learn about the different ways we could become parents. We couldn't do what so many of our straight friends had done – stop taking the pill / remove the coil / bin the johnnies, then shag more than usual and let nature take its course. If we'd left it to nature we would have ended up with friction burns and an empty crib. I envied the simplicity with which some of my straight friends got to approach creating a family. For LGBTQIA+ people it can be a long road to parenthood – buying sperm from across the globe, getting it shipped, paying for its hotel/storage, spending years finding a surrogate to help bring their child into the world or going through the adoption process. Every queer parent I know had huge, soul-baring conversations with their partner about how to start a family, where they should live so their kid has friends like them and whether they could afford the extra costs of creating a child in this way. For many of my friends, that cost is in the tens of thousands of pounds. It's heartbreaking to me when some people question whether LGBTQIA+ folk should be able to become parents, when we have to work so hard to get there. You have to really, really want a family to jump through the necessary hoops to get one.

We discovered that our options were assisted fertility in the form of IUI or IVF, or adoption. There's also at-home insemination but given how clumsy I am, we thought that wouldn't be for us. I'd be sure to trip and spill very expensive jizz on the bedroom rug (not a euphemism). IUI (intrauterine insemination) is a sort of pre-IVF, a procedure by which sperm is placed directly into the uterus via a catheter. With IVF (in-vitro fertilization) an egg – or more often, multiple eggs – is fertilized outside of the body in a lab. It involves hormone injections which cause the body to produce multiple eggs to maximize chances of success. Both techniques can be gruelling, painful and expensive but we had several friends who had successfully created families that way so we felt we at least had an understanding of the process. It felt hopeful and possible. We didn't know as much about adoption, but we soon learnt it could be just as gruelling as IVF when it came to how invasive it would be in our lives, as well as the myriad unknowns and the unpredictability that come with adopting a child.

We spent months discussing what felt right for us and, eventually, made our decision.

There were several moments when it felt like the life and the dream we were trying to create might never happen. There were sleepless nights. I would gently wiggle out of bed and pad down to the spare room which had become our imaginary child's bedroom. I'd sit on the armchair, the chair I had envisioned us snuggling up on to read *Hairy Maclary* and look at all the books and toys and teddies, things we'd bought too early, too hopefully, and I'd try to will our family into existence. I would look out the window and wish on the moon, like in a children's book I'd once read. I would talk to Nan's photo, much like she had spoken to my gramps: 'Nan, if there's anything you can do up there, please do it, make us a three.' Often Alice would find me asleep on the sofa and tenderly walk me back to bed.

Whether it was fate or the moon or my nan, we were lucky, so incredibly lucky and by the time I was thirty-five we *were* a three. A mummy, a mama and one little peach – given that nickname thanks to Alice's catchphrase, 'peachy'. Alice is generally upbeat and positive – she's the sort of kind and loving partner for whom nothing is too much trouble, and whenever you ask her how she's doing, nine times out of ten, her answer is: peachy. So our daughter's nickname was Peachy Peach, but you're right, that's too silly, so now she's just Peach. Which is a very sensible thing to shout across a park.

My daughter is adopted. It's something I haven't talked about until writing this. I wasn't sure whether to tell you, to be honest. Not because it's a secret but because it isn't my story to tell. It's hers and hers alone. For that reason, I'm not going to reveal any specific details, but I do find myself wanting to tell you about my experience of the process.

Having made the decision that adoption was our path we attended 'information evenings' with various adoption charities. We chose the one we wanted to work with, and kicked things off. To even be accepted formally as prospective adopters, we went through an invasive screening: probing, personal questions ranging from health to past trauma to how we were parented ourselves. Once we got through that, we began the 'training' process – attending courses with lots of other prospective adoptive parents. It was so interesting to see the cross-section of people wanting to adopt and the reasons that had led them there.

We were so pleased to find other LGBTQIA+ adopters: in fact the whole experience was incredibly inclusive. We gravitated to a couple of friendly, smiling gay guys of a similar age to us. Little did we know when we first met up over a cup of tea in a south London café, hopeful but a little anxious about the journey ahead, that in the not too distant future, we'd sit in their lounge, proper friends now, and look out into the garden to see their brilliant boys and our magnificent girl laughing and squealing as they pushed one another on a swing and ate ice cream to their hearts' content.

We were then assigned our utterly wonderful social

worker. We definitely couldn't have got through the process without her. This was where the harder work began, where we had to explore every moment of our lives and what had formed us to be the people we are today. We discussed every good, bad and ugly thing we'd experienced and then deconstructed how we could translate it into being the right type of parent to an adopted child. We had to evidence all of the reading we had done from the many brilliant books out there on adoption; we had to have medicals done to check our health; our finances were carefully examined (you don't have to have lots of money to adopt, they just need to make sure you aren't in huge debt, as that could have an impact on housing and security etc). Even ex-partners had to be contacted for character references.

It was full on. Adopting isn't easy but it shouldn't be. Children within the care system have already lost so much. They may have additional emotional or learning needs so it is imperative that their forever homes have been fully vetted and the prospective parents have the skills to support them and their needs.

The reason I wanted to share that our family has been made through adoption is because it's wonderful. Our child wasn't created by us in a fleeting moment of passion or in a fertility specialist's surgery. Our daughter was already in the world and her social worker was searching for the perfect family to love her. We were sent her profile the day we were approved to adopt. Then everything happened incredibly quickly. It fell into place, as if it had been preordained. If

I was a religious person I would say it was the will of God that we particular three ended up as a family but I prefer to think it was fate, something in the universe bringing us all together, because that was where we were always supposed to be. If I'd had a couple of glasses of wine, I would also say Nan might have chucked a bit of magic in too, but I haven't, so I won't.

We'd been warned in the adoption course not to expect love at first sight when you meet your child, that sometimes it takes weeks or even months to develop that connection. I know this can be true if you have a biological link too. You are, after all, strangers to each other. We drove for hours over hundreds of miles to reach her foster carer's place. Alice and I cuddled in the car before making our way to the flat, both of us, unusually, lost for words. I steadied myself as the foster carer opened the front door, with this beautiful little girl in her arms. Cupid's arrow hit me immediately. I was bowled over by love. She instantly put her arms out for us, like she knew us, like she'd been waiting for us to arrive. I looked into her eyes and thought: there you are. There's my daughter. I have been waiting for you too.

Over the years, when Alice and I have spoken about Peach's adoption to friends, family and colleagues, often they have responded: 'Oh, she's so lucky.' I know the sentiment is always coming from a kind place, and that what they are saying is: 'What a great kid, you're doing a good job,' but no child within the care system is 'lucky'; the fact that they are there at all means that part of their story has been very tragic and sad indeed. The truth is Alice and I are the lucky ones, we are the ones who hit the jackpot with this curious, interesting, clever, kind, loving and funny little person that we get to call our daughter. She is the person who made my dream of becoming a mama come true.

You can read all the books, buy adorable clothes and nod as your parent friends share their wisdom, but nothing can really prepare you for the moment when you walk through your front door with a child in your arms. I saw our reflection in the hallway mirror and knew that neither our home nor our life would ever be the same. I remember the first few months as a series of snapshots, rather than full days. I was scared for quite a lot of that period. My old friend, death anxiety, who I knew so well from my childhood, sneaked back. Often when I was in that syrupy place between sleeping and waking, I would have to jump up and check that this new person, this little girl that I loved so hard, so quickly, was OK, that she was happy, warm and settled.

Alice took a year of parental leave. I had a few months off to start with, then tried only to gig and take work in London. I quickly felt like the provider, even though we'd saved for a couple of years and Alice had maternity pay coming in. Peach came home during the pandemic, so I was doing these bizarre online gigs – literally performing stand-up into a laptop at my kitchen table – along with a little bit of writing work, and the occasional outdoor show. One particularly memorable occasion saw me on a stage, with the audience watching from inside their cars. Imagine an American-style drive-in movie but instead of watching Baby and Johnny do the mambo in *Dirty Dancing*, it was just me, miming a smear test to . . . silence. I don't know if people were laughing, they weren't allowed to open their windows. They also weren't allowed to toot their horns, so instead, when they liked a joke they'd flash their lights, like they were giving way. Giving way to me wondering what the fuck I was doing with my life. I felt like the warm-up act for a dogging event. But the pay was pretty good, so I went and earned that cash! In fact, when they offered me more shows I took them. Turns out I am pretty cheap and willing to lose all of my self-respect if there's a global pandemic on and I have a child at home.

Due to restrictions there were no IRL parent-and-baby classes, we could only take Peach out for an hour a day. None of our family or friends could come over and meet our new addition. It was just the three of us, 100 per cent of the time. And I loved it.

Much like Madonna we got into the groove. Without the constant, pre-2020 din of the outside world we had the time and space we needed to get used to being a family. It was ironic. The constant terrifying news briefings, confusing government instructions and understandable waves of fear that swept the country meant that all of a sudden the world and its wife had the kind of anxiety I had always lived with, but in our little Sydenham flat I felt a contentedness I had never before experienced. Outside was sometimes a different story.

Our daily walks were something to cherish: fresh air

and calm in the outside world. We'd get up and have breakfast together: Alice would get Peach ready while I showered, then I'd take her for a peaceful stroll while Alice took a moment to herself. A podcast in my ears, often Elizabeth Day's encouraging thoughts on failure, would be my company as I walked. I like walking, especially with a podcast I love. It resets me if I am feeling overwhelmed, which I was, often, unsurprisingly during a pandemic with a new daughter. But my equilibrium was often ruined, sometimes only minutes into my stroll. I'd become a woman who shouted at runners. I would always head to Beckenham Place Park, its glorious, rolling hills and thick forest, home to the most vibrant green and vocal parakeets. I would push her buggy pointing out squirrels and dogs along the way. The park was usually empty, the streets too. At any other time the quiet would have seemed odd, eerie even, but it had somehow become normal. Then, I would see on the pavement ahead of me a jogger, running towards me, sweating, panting, huffing in a way that told me he was, at the very least, an occasional vaper. As he got closer I assumed he would step into the very empty road to go around us and give us some room. But no. He huffed, puffed and spluttered his way past us, close enough to gently brush my arm. No. I wasn't having it.

'Are you fucking kidding me?'

'What?' he replied, taking out one earphone.

'We are meant to be keeping two metres between us. There's a global pandemic on and she is a very little girl with a minimal immune system.'

He laughed at me and jogged off. His laughter sent me mad. He made me feel stupid, but I wasn't stupid, I was an anxious new mum trying to dodge Covid. I cried in the street but that sort of angry cry that makes you feel like a child who can't control their emotions (which upsets you even more). I stormed home to the safety of our little flat, thinking of ways I could hunt this man down and give him a piece of my mind. I would fantasize about turning up on his doorstep and coughing directly in his face, but I didn't really have the confidence or the resources for that; it's also really rude and what if I accidentally actually gave him Covid and he lived with an elderly relative and I killed her. I couldn't have that on my conscience, I haven't got the stomach for murder. So instead I just sulked around our flat, winding myself up and frequently muttering under my breath: 'What a bloody selfish, thoughtless wanker.' Alice gently asked if I was feeling more anxious than usual and wondered if I was maybe overreacting a little. I agreed I probably was.

But, as 2021 rolled around, it brought a sense of calm and hope. I was feeling more confident as a mum and hardly ever shouted at strangers exercising.

Progress.

But it wasn't only joggers who could set me off. Social media was a culprit too.

One particular morning, I was trying to relax, sitting in the armchair with the sun pouring through the window, munching on a cheese-and-cucumber sandwich. It turns out I have inherited my mother's deep desire to make sandwiches constantly. I was scrolling on my phone while Peach was snoozing in her bedroom next door.

It had been a tricky morning. Restrictions had been lifted and we'd been on our way to Rhyme Time at the local library (thank God for local libraries) when Peach sharted with such force that her whole outfit was in immediate desperate need of a hot wash. I nipped into the library baby change and realized I had left her changing bag, packed and ready, on the sofa at home, a thirty-minute walk away. I panicked and then I burst into tears. I didn't know what else to do. Peach cried too. Hers a livid wail, mine a gentle sob. This was so typically me. So clichéd. So unsurprising. I hadn't left enough time to get to the class, so I had jogged most of the way there, not like the actual jogging parents in Lycra who have those three-wheeler buggies that scream: I am smashing parenting so hard I have excess energy to burn. Pricks. I had jogged in baggy jeans, some Doc Martens that weren't fully broken in and a puffer coat. I had sweat dripping down my back. I hoped I'd put on deodorant, but I really couldn't swear to it.

The previous night, I'd been in Peach's room to comfort her five times. So when the alarm went off (the alarm in this scenario is her shouting for us) I had to peel myself off the mattress and pour coffee directly into my eyes.

Alice would never have forgotten the bag. If Alice was here Peach would already be changed, fresh and bopping along to 'Five Little Ducks Went Swimming One Day' but on this particular day, no little ducks were swimming, one was covered in excrement and Mama Duck was crying while berating herself behind the locked door of the public library baby change. In that moment I felt like such a rubbish mum. Embarrassed and ashamed. I felt I had really let Peach down. So, no Rhyme Time – her favourite activity of the week – for us today. We had to get home as quickly as possible. I started jogging back, the Doc Martens now *really* rubbing – I could feel the heel of my sock filling with blood. We covered the half-hour walk home in twelve minutes (maybe those jogging mums are on to something) and, soon after, Peach was out of the bath, fresh, clean and slightly less livid. She absolutely yummed down a cream cheese sandwich, and now she was snoozing happily. After a nap, I felt sure we'd have a better afternoon, one where I'd feel less like I had failed her. The blister on my heel had popped. It was red and furious. Whatever we were doing this afternoon I'd be wearing sliders.

So, trying to recover some equilibrium, to maybe be a little less harsh on myself, I sat in my armchair, and tried to relax. I was scrolling Instagram aimlessly, when I came across a post from a mid-tier celebrity, who has a kid of a similar age to Peach. They were out for a walk, she looked radiant, and they were both in beige. BEIGE! With a child under three? I look like I haven't slept in a week (because I haven't) and I couldn't be trusted in beige before I had a kid. Under the picture-perfect post she wrote: I know people won't like me for saying this but motherhood is coming to me so easily, I feel like it's the job I have been waiting for. Kisses. Her writing 'Kisses' made me want to throw up. All my familiar feelings of deficiency returned with a bang. Clearly I wasn't good enough, for Alice or for my daughter. Who was that post even for? It felt like it was a personal slight aimed directly at me. I assume it wasn't, in part because I have actually been reintroduced to this woman twice without her remembering she's met me and if we met again I would bet we'd have a hat-trick. What was her intention? To let others know she was smashing it, while being fully aware that many of us won't feel like we are? Was she never told not to brag? I did what I often do in those scenarios, I called my friend and old housemate Jenny. These days we saved each other in our phones as Reassurance Hotline. Anxiety has underscored her life too so we have an acute understanding of one another's hot pangs of panic and while I am sure that in a way we facilitate the angst we share, it is good to have a friend to whom you can comfortably say: Am I being mental? And find relief in the answer either way. Jenny, however, said that I wasn't being mental and as a new mum herself too, she understood exactly where I was coming from. She reminded me that social media isn't real and that it is in fact damaging society beyond measure. She'd recently ditched all her social media accounts and was feeling heaps better. Post phone call I felt my heart rate return to somewhere closer to normal.

Forty-five minutes later Peach woke up jolly, totally unaware that Mama had experienced an existential crisis about her ability to parent during her forty winks. It wasn't a one-off. I overthought everything from what to feed her and the correct bath temperature, to every cough and sneeze. I constantly needed Alice's reassurance, and even after calling the Reassurance Hotline, Kisses continued to make me feel a whole lot more self-conscious and unsure of myself.

Over the next few weeks I thought of that 'celebrity' often. Every time I didn't feel good enough, her voice would pop into my head: Motherhood is coming to me so easily, I feel like it's the job I have been waiting for. But then, a couple of months later, I was shooting a panel show. I was chatting to the make-up lady, Hannah, who mentioned she'd worked with Kisses a few weeks earlier. I made some joke about my face being a bigger job – a comment about the bags under my eyes and the stress eczema breakout on my forehead. It was a half-apologetic/half-shame-faced request for a boost about my appearance and I followed it up with: 'Her daughter is a similar age to mine. She's smashing it, but I feel like I'm hanging on by a thread.'

'Well,' Hannah replied as she leant in, conspiratorially. 'She has a full-time nanny, a husband, and her mum has moved in. It's four to one.'

Then she gave me a little shoulder squeeze, a shoulder squeeze I really needed. Now, I am not knocking having help, Lord knows I will take all I can get, but pretending that motherhood is 'easy' while someone else is doing the nights is a bloody piss-take. It also perpetuates this myth that having it all is not only what we all should be striving for but also achievable. Kisses has a stellar career. It made

185

me wonder what had made her feel the need to omit part of the truth. Were there impossible standards laid on her shoulders? Was she lying to herself too? I have been guilty of posting a picture looking great when I felt like shit and allowing those little love heart likes to gently massage my fragile ego. Perhaps that's what she was doing too, not thinking of how it might make others reading her post feel.

The problem was, I was feeling a *lot* all of the time. Now, friends, we are at Chapter 8 so we all know that big feelings aren't a new thing for me but now they were different, because I knew that I was holding Peach's future in my hands. Before Peach, I'd read a lot of books on early-years development and attachment. Knowing that we didn't have a biological link to her I wanted to make sure we did absolutely everything to ensure she felt connected to us both. In reading those books I realized how important early childhood is. I was hyper-aware of everything we fed her, of how much she slept. We limited any kind of screen time or sugar because of a conversation I had with a paediatrician about brain development. I wanted to give her the best chance possible. Even if some of the people around us found our dismissal of sugary treats and *Peppa Pig* an irritation, and our strict guidelines on nap times and bedtime tiresome, we were happy to make our life a bit harder for a while in order for her to have the best chance possible in the long run.

Firstly, there is a privilege I must address here. I know not every parent has the time that we had in order to adhere to our chosen parenting style. I am also acutely aware that because Peach is an only child, we could put all of our energies into her alone. You might be reading this and thinking we went over the top. Indeed, you might have read something that contradicts exactly what I am saying. There is a lot of conflicting information when it comes to parenting, some more relaxed, some with an emphasis on learning, some with the emphasis on play, some with an emphasis on child-led activity, and that's all before you consider the location you live in and the type of school your child will attend. In all corners of the world people are parenting in totally different ways, utterly convinced that their way is right. We just found the way that made the most sense to us.

Alice and I had quite different experiences growing up. Her parents were stricter than mine, and they considered her school work particularly important. My parents wanted me to behave at school but they weren't at all pushy when it came to exams or homework. They didn't think of me as especially academically gifted, so as long as I didn't cause too much trouble they were happy. They knew my school days were a lonely experience and they put so much effort into my after-school activities, my mum ferrying me around town several nights a week for my hobbies. They were as hopeful as me that I could one day muddle a career out of them.

This meant that when it came to parenting, Alice and I were singing from quite different song sheets. It was important we found a middle ground that suited us both and made us feel confident in our parenting skills. As Peach grew up we didn't want to constantly play good cop and bad cop, we wanted to be a united front. We also felt that boundaries were the key to a child feeling settled and happy.

When Peach started nursery we had a whole new load of obstacles to deal with – one of the most pressing being other people's parenting styles making their way into our home. 'Nancy is allowed her iPad every night before bed,' 'Billy uses his scooter on the main road,' 'Annie's mum lets her have a big chocolate bar every single day.' I wondered how many of these claims were actually true, as well as how to answer these new demands without causing a tantrum from the brutal unfairness of only giving Peach a little bit of chocolate, an iPad occasionally and only allowing her to scoot in areas where there was no moving traffic.

And that's before you consider the tantrums.

Peach's first mega tantrum hit when we were in a Robert Dyas buying a new mop. As we were queuing to pay she clocked the items on special surrounding the till. She pointed at a box. 'I want it, I want it, I want it.' 'It' was an air fryer. She didn't know it was an air fryer, or what air frying is – she just liked the look of the box and wanted to take it home. I tried to reason with her but she wouldn't have it. She wept and railed against me, climaxing with a full body slam on to the floor, but obviously I didn't give in, firstly because you can't just give in to them, and secondly because we already have an air fryer (that we bought with the best intentions and have only used twice). I let people walk around us as I held her hand and she wrestled with the unfairness of the world (to a toddler who wasn't allowed an air fryer).

You can't reason with kids, that's what I have learnt. You have to just accept that they can't regulate their emotions which means sometimes they are awful; not that you love them any less, but they are occasionally self-obsessed, demanding divas with no understanding that life exists outside of them. Much like a comedian (myself included) at the Edinburgh Festival. All you can do is allow them their emotions and offer them a cuddle when they are finished with all the screaming (much like a comedian at the Edinburgh Festival).

And I fear that we aren't even at the hard bit yet, navigating school, friendship groups, puberty, her as a teen, social media. I worry about what's to come. One of my wishes for Peach is that she worries a bit less than I do.

I am convinced that anxiety runs in my family. I have crystal-clear memories of my nan overreacting, with her head in her hands, as I scuttled up climbing frames or swam out so far in the sea I would just hear her shouting from the shoreline: 'Come back, Suz, you're going to bloody drown.' I remember the look of sheer panic on her face, it's the same look Mum has now when Peach jumps in a swimming pool or goes down a ten-foot slide face first. I can't be sure whether that's nature or nurture but either way I really don't want Peach to receive that trait. A sense of humour, a love of the seaside, a childlike excitement for Christmas that withstands well into her thirties: Yes, please. The sleepless nights, the overthinking, the dread that you might have done the wrong thing (when really you know you haven't). No, thank you, not for her.

I want to keep her safe but allow her to be adventurous, to

try her best but not be heartbroken by failure, to be loving but not a walkover. I want to give her the skills for life without her getting sick of my suggestions. I just want her to be happy but is that a lot of pressure to put on a child? I need help.

. . .

So I sat down with Dr Martha Deiros Collado, clinical psychologist and author of *How to Be the Grown-up: Why good parenting starts with you.*

Firstly I wanted to know whether anxious parents make anxious children.

'Great question. The short answer is no.'

A huge relief!

'What we know from research is that anxious parents don't make anxious children, but anxious parents sometimes teach children unhelpful strategies around anxiety.

'When I work with children and their families, the most powerful thing a parent with anxiety can do is learn strategies that are helpful to manage anxiety and to explicitly talk about them and pass them on to their kids. So use anxiety as an opportunity to support your child in developing a toolkit, whether they have anxiety or not. Because anxiety is part of life, right? We all experience anxiety, your children are going to have anxiety. It's normal. It's a normal emotion. And rather than being scared of it or feeling helpless, we can teach our children: sometimes I'm anxious, but this is what I do that helps me.

'And then when they feel anxious, they're like: oh, my mum said, or my dad said, that I could do this.'

Like a breathing exercise or something like that?

'Exactly. And just naming it.'

My body is always such a giveaway. My daughter immediately notices my shoulders going up when she does something that panics me, but rather than putting on a brave face, maybe I should just be honest with her.

'When my daughter was little in the playground, I didn't like her going on the monkey bars,' Martha confides. 'They're really high up and they genuinely made me feel really anxious. I'm not a chill parent in the playground. So I just told her, I said: I don't like it when you are on the monkey bars because my body feels really scared that you're going to fall. And I *know* you're safe. But my body's saying you're not safe. So when it's just you and me at the playground, let's do slides, swings, all these other fun things and then at the weekend, when your daddy's here, you can do the monkey bars.'

I love that advice – the openness and honesty of it. A related thing I find hard, I tell Martha, is the contradiction between wanting my daughter to have the freedom to grow and learn and make mistakes but to be safe at all times, too.

'First of all, I think you need to work on yourself, which is the hardest task of all, right? You need to allow your child to take safe risks. So the monkey bars is a great example. I needed to allow her to do the monkey bars, albeit when I wasn't there! And now she's older, I *can* be there with her. So, we've grown together with the risk.

'Because now she's a bigger kid, she's going to be all right, even if she falls. But when she was little, I really struggled with it. You need to find the balance. Allow your child a safe risk, and if you don't think it's safe, tell your child. Just be honest about it.

'We have to allow our children to take safe risks because that's where they learn and also that's where resilience is born. Resilience isn't born by getting things right all the time. It comes when we make mistakes, when we trip up. So we need to allow our children to fail. We need to allow our children to feel disappointed. We need to allow our children to fall over. And to then offer them safety. It's not about reassurance. Safety is about saying: you fell and that really hurt. But I'm here for you. Right?'

I am someone who seeks and gives a lot of reassurance but Martha suggested I might need a different approach.

'Reassurance can actually be really unhelpful. If you are constantly telling your child: everything is OK, you're fine, you'll have a better day tomorrow, next time you'll make the football team, it's risky. You can't be certain of any of those things. As parents we are just being hopeful. We need to stop telling kids that we're going to fix it or that it's going to get better. Actually, sometimes children and adults just need to hear: this is shit.

'And if you're telling them, for example, that next time they will make the football team and they don't, they might end up experiencing double the disappointment because they may feel they've let their parent down too. Resilience comes from the place of: I messed up, and it hurt me somehow, physically or emotionally, and I got through it.

I think people get that really confused. Someone might say that a child's not resilient, because they cried when they messed up or they fell over. But you need to allow the emotion.

'If the kid falls over and hurts themselves, cries, gets some support from an adult and then runs off again, that's resilience. If the kid messes up on a test and cries in class, but then carries on with their day, that's resilience.'

I wondered how strict Martha is as a mum, with her years of experience and knowledge.

'To me, strict means firm,' she explains. 'I think that's a better word. I talk in my work a lot about firm boundaries. There's like a set of rules or limits, and we keep them firmly but I hope, and you'd have to ask my children, I'm warm and empathic with it.'

I agree that firm is a better word, and I've learnt that you have to have some areas that are firm and some that are more flexible, so the child doesn't feel caged in.

'My daughter is five and a half, and I choose what she eats. She doesn't choose. And there's no alternatives. Some parents would say: oh no, I wouldn't do that. I need my child to eat. But I trust that she will eat, because I'm not so harsh that I'm going to give her a plate of food of something she's never seen. I know she likes the things on her plate. We are firm on screens. So my daughter doesn't really watch screens. She will play on the iPad sometimes, like on the weekend. And she has a drawing game. But she can't just sit on it for hours. We're firm on shopping, so toys and gift shops. So I will tell her, if we're going to the aquarium and there's a gift shop: We're not buying any toys today because the treat is the aquarium.

'She sometimes says: Can I look around but I know we're not buying anything – and she's fine. She's so used to that boundary, she's prepared. I'll say things like: We can take a photo if you like, and then when it's your birthday or Christmas, if you still remember the toy and still want it, we've got a photo. So now she'll sometimes say: I don't want to buy it today, but can we take a photo?'

I love that. I am using that! And it must give her daughter ownership of the situation as well. She understands it.

'Exactly. And around birthdays and Christmases, I'll sometimes ask her: do you need some ideas for grandparents and aunties? What about looking at all these photos? Which of these do you remember? She remembers some of them vividly. And it also teaches delayed gratification, which is really important. It's all about preparing our kids; helping them. All the scientific research says that permissiveness is not helpful.'

So boundaries are good?

'Absolutely. So even though kids push against them, that's what they're supposed to do. That's part of their development, particularly like as they get older. Teenagers push against boundaries a lot. It's part of the process. It doesn't mean you've got it wrong as a parent.'

This idea of pushing away from your parents as a teenager really chimes with what Natasha Devon told me back in Chapter 2, talking about whether peaking at high school ruins you for life.

'If you don't give any boundaries, you just allow your kid to do what they want, how they want, it's really unhealthy for them. It makes children feel unsafe and it doesn't teach them the things that we often want to teach them. Another firm one for us is about kindness and respect.

'So we say to our daughter, kindness and respect is a really important value for us. She does sometimes speak to us with a sassy voice. Already, at five, she'll say: I don't want that, and I'll say: Try that again and say it nicely because I can hear you but you don't have to talk to me like that. We try and model it. And she'll also say something similar to us, sometimes: 'I don't like the way you talk to me.' Those are the times when I know I'm doing something right. I want her to feel able to say that to me, too.

'After all, parenting is a two-way relationship. This is the difference between strict and firm. In a strict household, you might say that's your child talking back. But for me, it's not her talking back. It's her telling me our relationship is safe enough that I can tell you when I don't really like how you talk to me.'

I'm kind of relieved to hear that sometimes Martha, for all her expertise, might not always get it right, and talks to her daughter in a way that she doesn't like. I ask her what tips she has for parents when we get things wrong.

'Apologize,' she tells me. 'Meaningfully. People really struggle with this. Lots of adults don't know how to apologize.

'"I'm sorry" is just the beginning of an apology. It's about really owning your behaviour, not excusing it. So it's not: I'm sorry I shouted at you, but you weren't listening to me. No, that's not an apology. It's: I'm sorry I shouted at you because I got angry and it's not OK for me to shout.

'*That's* an apology. A lot of the time, a meaningful apology comes with accountability, with a sense of: I'm going to work on this. Or: I know I shout when I'm angry. It's something I learnt when I was a kid. That's how my parents were around me, but I'm trying really hard to do something different and I'm sorry that sometimes I still mess up.

'Learning how to apologize properly to my child has taught me how to apologize to my husband. And he and I have a much more honest and a stronger relationship because of that. That's really important because we're teaching our children how to repair with us and how to repair with others. And we're teaching children that as a human you can mess up, but your relationship doesn't have to break down.'

I can't tell you how relieved I was when I got off this call with Martha. It gave me a lot of hope that my anxiety won't be a foregone conclusion for Peach. It also reminded me that having anxiety and dealing with it in positive ways are good messages for me to convey to Peach as she grows up. I can show her that she too will be able to cope with any curveball life throws her way.

It's good to remember that as parents we can get things wrong. We don't need to be able to wear beige and not get it stained, whatever people like Kisses may show us on social media. Accountability is more important than perfection;

making mistakes and learning from them and repairing rifts will give your child more helpful life lessons than a parent who is constantly trying to get everything perfect.

CHAPTER 9

Has LGBTQIA+ equality been achieved?

No.

(Well, that was a short chapter.)

Let me put it another way:

Is life improving for your local neighbourhood queer person?

OK, let's get stuck in.

If I somehow acquired a time machine, I'd travel back to the 1950s and head straight to London's Gateways Club. The Gates, as it was affectionately known, was London's first (recorded) lesbian bar. It opened in 1931 and didn't serve its final pint until Saturday 21 September 1985. Tucked behind a little green door on the King's Road in Chelsea, it was a safe haven for queer people, curious heterosexuals and members of any other minority group experiencing discrimination. During its Swinging Sixties heyday the private members' bar hosted stars like Diana Dors and Dusty Springfield and legend has it Mick Jagger was refused entry on more than one occasion.

I think a lot about the people who must have visited the Gates, London's premier spot for queer women. Did they live their whole lives in secret? In fear? Were they, in fact, forced to lead double lives? Maybe some were in lavender marriages, where a gay man and a lesbian become a 'couple' to keep people off the scent (the gay scent: clean linen, fresh flowers and poppers). I feel a connection to these people I have never met, a kinship perhaps, an understanding. While I have no physical link to them, when I look at pictures of queer people from history it's like looking at photos of family members I never met. I recognize something of myself in them. Although I only know how it felt to come out to a loving family in the early 2000s, in a country that was pretty tolerant and where there are no laws preventing me from being open about my sexuality, I still found it an enormous feat. I can only imagine how terrifying it must have been to face that back in the fifties. While they wouldn't have been staring lovingly at Kate Winslet in the ABC Picture House Portsmouth (for the seventh time), I imagine the feeling of otherness, the fear (and yes, the excitement) might have been the same. And whilst there were no legal ramifications to lesbianism, male homosexuality was illegal in the UK until 1967, and it wasn't unusual for gay women to be subjected to the horrors of electric shock therapy or committed to an asylum.

In that world, I can imagine the thrill of being surrounded by people who really see you. I know the need to spend time with people who really understand and have experienced your journey. I remember that feeling when Tom Allen and I met at a comedy gig more than ten years ago. We became good friends very quickly. We shared a quiet and considerate understanding, an 'I get it'. Spending time with my lesbian friends is something I cherish. I think it soothes the lonely teenage me, the girl who thought she was unacceptable, who assumed at some level that she'd live a lonely life. It heals the part that was drenched in shame and guilt. In their company there's an ease, a contentment. In its simplest explanation, it feels like home.

So as well as perhaps looking for love I would guess women at the Gates were also searching for companionship and understanding. I imagine these women – brave enough to seek out a place like the Gates but most likely living undercover, potentially cut off from family – might have fantasized about a life like mine, a life lived outside the closet.

What would one of them, a fictional 1950s lesbian – let's call her Bette, she's drinking a gin fizz and wearing a sharp, tailored suit – think of me? That I live with my partner, that we own property together, that we are married in the eyes of the law, that we share a surname, that we have a daughter. That not only do my family know the truth about me but that I tell hundreds, sometimes thousands, of people about it onstage several times a week.

Bette would assume we'd fixed it – she'd think equality had been achieved and it was time to open the champagne. But sadly, I would have to urge her to pop that cork back in the bottle. Even a light scratch of the surface reveals we have a long, long way to go.

As of January 2024, thirty-six countries recognized same-sex marriage, which sounds OK (as long as you happen to live in one) until you remember there are one hundred and ninety-five countries in the world. Consensual same-sex sexual acts have the death penalty in Mauritania, Saudi Arabia, Somalia, the United Arab Emirates, Iran and

Afghanistan. Only a few years ago in the Russian Federation of Chechnya there was a police campaign labelled the 'gay purge' where queer people were rounded up in the streets and taken to camps. Many are still missing as I write this today. Uganda passed a law in 2014, which was previously dubbed the Kill the Gays bill, which encourages people to share information on friends and family if you suspect they might be engaging in same-sex acts. Hiding such information could have you thrown into prison too. Homosexuality is illegal in sixty-four countries, with punishment being anything from two years to life imprisonment, ten years of hard labour to one hundred lashes. So I think we can all agree that things aren't 'fixed' for you or your queer pals just yet.

That's not to say that progress hasn't been made – it has, in some places at least. But even where rights have been won, rights for which the queers who came before me fought so hard, they're now being infringed. At the time of writing, the British government still hasn't banned conversion therapy; LGBTQIA+ hate crime is on the rise in the UK; the Italian government has removed same-sex couples from birth certificates; Russia has effectively outlawed the LGBTQIA+ 'movement'; Florida has introduced a Section 28-style 'Don't Say Gay' bill. This is all before we consider the lives of our trans and non-binary siblings which are picked apart daily in both the courts and the media.

Things suddenly feel less hopeful than they did a few years ago. There was a glorious moment in 2015 when the people of Ireland voted overwhelmingly to legalize same-sex marriage. I remember watching a clip and bawling my eyes out. I am not even 2 per cent Irish so it wasn't due to any affinity with the place but because it was Europe's first ever same-sex marriage legislation to be actually voted in by the people, and that happening somewhere where religion is very high on the political agenda felt like a joyful turning point.

By 2022, it felt like we were turning back.

I'd taken my morning walk to a café I loved which did an excellent breakfast bagel (scrambled egg, spinach and hollandaise sauce) and I knew if I timed it correctly, Peach might have fallen asleep in her buggy by the time we arrived. A bagel, a coffee and a few chapters of a book. Perfect. It was autumn, cold but dry and the sun was still making welcome cameos throughout the day. I walked down the waterway link. We stopped to feed a little collection of ducks and moorhens, via the park where Peach had her daily ride on the swings, and as I pushed the café door open Peach was in a deep enough sleep that the whoosh and growl of the coffee machine wouldn't wake her and I knew if the wind blew in my favour I would have an hour of me time. A treat! I ordered and found a table, cluttered with detritus from its previous occupant: a free magazine, a coffee cup, a plate with the crumbs of a scone and a leaflet. As I waited for my bagel I absent-mindedly read the leaflet, a flyer for someone running for a local council election.

I felt it like a punch in the gut: *We need to return to a Christian way of life, we need the return of traditional family values.* The messaging was furious, blatant homophobia, suggesting that LGBTQIA+ people were damaging society.

She wanted local schools to lose books that featured LGBTQIA+ families, suggesting it was confusing and unnecessary for children. She believed children learning about people like me was a form of child abuse. She believed that the acceptance of families that didn't fit the Christian way of life – one mother, one father and Sunday trips to church – ensured a one-way ticket to the fiery pits of hell.

My eyes pricked with tears. I had felt safe, living in one of the most cosmopolitan cities in the world, married to another woman, able to be a family. Of course, I knew there will always people who feel this way about people like me, but to read it on a pamphlet for a prospective local councillor – someone hoping to be part of the establishment – while waiting for my cappuccino felt like a slap.

I love London. By then, I'd lived there for seventeen years but, increasingly, I'd seen queer pals with kids in the capital and other big cities face issues I naively hadn't expected. It made me wise up. These are places where you'd assume open-mindedness. But in some areas parents were withdrawing their children for a day if the school celebrated Pride. There were school gates protests against books in the school library featuring same-sex parents. If those parents believed their children were too young to know that same-sex families exist, what would that mean for mine? Would we have to pretend we were invisible until Peach's classmates reached the age they could finally know about us?

That prospective councillor didn't get voted in, but she did find support in parts of the community. It was sobering.

Being a family has cast a light on both the everyday

homophobia that LGBTQIA+ people face here, in one of the most privileged nations for queer people on earth, and in the rest of the world, too.

On the whole, I feel safe in the UK. There *are* places my wife and I wouldn't hold hands – occasionally because it feels unsafe, more often because we can't be bothered with the attention – but in the main it's fine. Going abroad is a whole different story.

I like the beach – I love completely submerging myself in clear blue sea while the sun beats down, making everything around me glisten; I don't mind sand providing a free exfoliation to areas I didn't know wanted to be scrubbed after a day at the beach. I love trying local cuisine, witnessing local customs and cultures, and hearing nothing but the gentle whoosh of the sea as it lazily draws in and out while I'm deep in a romance novel. I love walking around an old market square and hearing the hubbub of a language and a life that isn't mine.

My favourite person to travel with is Alice. As you might be able to imagine from previous chapters Alice is the planner and I am the one who once lost her passport until the morning of the flight only to find it down the side of a sofa. I am also the one who once left my house keys in a safe in Portugal and had to climb through a very small bathroom window upon my return. I am quite fun though (she writes hopefully). On holiday Alice and I are regularly assumed to be sisters, despite the fact that we look nothing alike and are sometimes holding hands. I assume the hotel staff considering us to be sisters is far more comfortable for them than confronting the truth: we are Doc Martenwearing, Sarah Waters-reading, Brandi Carlile-listening, Wanda Sykes-loving, full-time lesbians. They would sooner assume that the reason we both have the surname Ruffell is because we are sisters who bear absolutely no physical resemblance to one another than a couple of birds in love.

In 2018 when we travelled to India and Sri Lanka, it was much safer to lean into the sister trope than risk dealing with the outcome of the truth. On one trip I pretended our gay friend Trevor was my husband. I am quite boyish and Trevor is a very attractive, very preened and polished gay man. It felt like we were performing a farce: imagine if k.d. lang and RuPaul introduced themselves as a happily married couple. We all laughed about it at the time, Trevor and I playing it up for our friends' amusement. He shouted: 'There's my wife!' as I strutted towards him in Birkenstocks and a Topman shirt. Even though we all had the giggles there was a sadness in the pit of my stomach throughout our role-play at the fact that we had to pretend to be other people, that our true selves weren't enough and, of course, fear that people would find out who we really were.

It can feel upsetting and unpleasant to visit countries where lesbians are seen as criminals or mentally unwell but I never wanted other people's narrow-mindedness to stop me from seeing the world. It helped that I always knew we had our return flights home. I would always breathe a sigh of relief as the plane took off, knowing I was going back to a place where I could be me. So many people aren't so lucky. Looking out of the aeroplane windows I always felt so much for the queer people who called those countries home, who don't have a return flight to safety. I wondered how they lived, how they loved, what their lives looked like. It's especially sobering when leaving countries that have outdated laws because of colonial rule. It feels unbelievably cruel that laws made by the UK, a place which has since dispensed with such rules, are still destroying LBGTQIA+ people's lives in parts of the globe that the British Empire invaded.

Before we were parents, I could laugh off the thoughtless comments, the wild assumptions, the out-and-out homophobia. But as soon as we were a three I simply couldn't have it any more. I didn't want my daughter to think there are ever circumstances where we pretend we're not who we are. I don't want her to grow up feeling that our family is wrong or not good enough, wherever in the world we happen to be. I don't want her to know that many people across the globe object to us, that some think we are at best a fad and at worst dangerous, disgusting criminals. Surely I can keep her safe from other people's prejudice until she's in double figures.

We thought we were playing it safe when we went to Greece, on our first family holiday. We chose Greece because it's a country where same-sex marriage is legal (and also because it's the homeland of Sappho, the poet who officially invented lesbians, or was at least the first person to take the time to write about them in between all the girl-on-girl action). We wanted a family trip where we could be ourselves. Plenty of countries with homophobic laws boast gorgeous holiday destinations, and I understand that hotel and resort staff in those places tend to 'look the other way' when it comes to LGBTQ+ tourists. But I don't want to visit them. I don't want to be given different treatment from that which is endured by the queer people who actually have to live in these places. And, frankly, I don't want to spend my hard-earned cash to support the economies of nations that outlaw and punish homosexuality. I wanted our first family holiday to be perfect. (Little side note to new parents who are yet to have their first family holiday: a holiday with a toddler IS NOT a holiday. It's a feat of endurance, testing you physically and mentally, an obstacle course of pools, playgrounds and sleep deprivation. Like a tough mudder. A tough mother if you will.)

As soon as we arrived, we felt a vibe, and it wasn't a good one. The staff looked suspiciously at our little family, at our tired daughter clutching Mama and then asking for Mummy. We noticed the reception staff sharing glances. I knew quickly this wasn't going to be the perfect holiday we'd dreamt of. Right from the first day by the pool we felt out of place. We weren't being touchy feely (unlike plenty of the straight couples nearby) but we operate like a family, because we *are* a family. One Russian couple with several children were fascinated by us: they openly stared and sneered, and were clearly talking about us. Now, I am not at all familiar with the language but it wasn't hard to know how they felt when they ostentatiously moved their kids away from us. After a couple of hours of uncomfortable judgement we moved, too: we didn't want to be near their hate. For the majority of the holiday no other families spoke to us. I was desperate to find a little playmate for Peach but it didn't happen. We'd booked an all-inclusive hotel, one with activities and a beach, thinking: that'll be great, we won't even have to leave the hotel unless we go on a day trip, when in reality we couldn't wait to get away. One day, at great expense, we hired a car to go and see some peacocks just to escape for a few hours. You can choose a country that on the face of it seems to be pro-gay but you can't choose the hotel staff or your fellow holidaymakers. For the whole week we felt judged and out of place. One night while Alice and Peach slept I googled flights home, desperate to get back to the safe embrace of Brighton.

Yup, that's right, we now live in Brighton, LGBTQIA+ capital of the UK.

The incident with the councillor was the catalyst for moving from South London to the UK's gayest city, but it had always been the long-term plan. We'd always thought that if we were lucky enough to become parents, we didn't want to live somewhere where we would be tolerated, just put up with. We wanted to live somewhere where we would feel equal. I also loved the idea of being the type of person that sea-swims, wears a dry robe and owns a paddle board. I wanted to find a community, a hub that accepted us fully.

I grew up feeling like an outsider and the last thing I wanted for my daughter was to feel that she was different because of us. And that doesn't mean we only wanted to hang with other gay families – some of my best friends are straight – but we knew that Brighton was overwhelmingly pro-gay and that schools, teachers and other parents would be used to families like ours.

London is a very diverse place to live, and that's one of

the many reasons I loved it but, sadly, we found that some sections of that diversity did a disservice to ours. This has always utterly baffled me. When I have received hate or threats from someone who is also from a marginalized community, surely there's an understanding of otherness that we could connect over. Surely respecting and accepting each other would be beneficial to us both? Surely we could be each other's allies in the fight for equality?

The week we moved into our Brighton house the other double-mum family on our street left home-made cupcakes on the doorstep, with a card to welcome us. Within the first couple of months we learnt about the local rainbow families group that have meet-ups several times a year. We found a primary school that understood our family. We found our community. And I got a paddle board.

It strikes me now that I ran to Brighton for acceptance the same way I ran to London nearly twenty years before. Perhaps you're reading this as an LGBTQIA+ parent in a big city, and maybe you've experienced some of the issues I've mentioned. I can see how you might think I am a coward for running away. I'm aware of having a level of financial privilege that allows me to relocate. I'm grateful for that. But nobody should have to move to feel comfortable with who they are, and with the kind of family they create. Perhaps someone who was brave, maybe Bette and her friends from the Gates, wouldn't have moved to a lefty liberal bubble, to an area known for its large queer population. I can see how you might think that the only way real change happens is when people stand up to bullies rather than run away, that

I live in an echo chamber, and in many ways I know you're right but being a public-facing queer person I have received more than my fair (fair?) share of homophobia over the years whether onstage or via social media. A handful of times I have received quite frightening physical threats and every time I was happy to stand my ground, to give two fingers to the bullies, to continue to be unapologetically myself. I could take it. But when the hate came for families like ours, when it was about Peach too, I was done with the bullies. I didn't want to give their hate the air time or the brain space, I knew my anxiety couldn't take it. So I ran to a gay haven by the seaside for my girls and my mental health.

Perhaps you're reading this thinking I am asking for too much. You might be thinking: Suz, chill, mate, you've got the marriage and the kid, you gays just want too much, and to you, firstly, I would say: I'm amazed you've got this far through the book. But secondly I'd ask: is wanting the same, too much? Is basic equality a step too far? Why should I be grateful for breadcrumbs of acceptance? Why should I feel grateful that discrimination is less than it used to be, but still there? As the brilliant Owen O'Kane, who I spoke to in Chapter 3, pointed out, being a queer often means knowing shame. A happy life can mean unpicking that prejudice and probable internalized homophobia from your early life, but let me tell you, once you've unpicked it, once you've accepted who you are, and when you're finally in a place where you're able to celebrate yourself, there's no fucking way you're going back.

So I guess I'd tell Bette that things will improve greatly, that there will be places in the world where we are accepted, pockets where we are celebrated. I'd tell her about Pride marches, marriage equality, Alan Turing, the great love story of Sarah Paulson and Holland Taylor. About Drag Race, about female footballers celebrating their goals by kissing their girl-friends in the crowd in front of millions on TV. About same-sex couples on *Strictly Come Dancing*, about me out onstage and making people laugh regardless of their sexuality. I would tell her about dancing with my gay girls at Brighton Pride in short shorts and a rainbow crop top and Alice throwing her arm around me and kissing me on the lips for everyone to see. I'd tell her about the joy of my weird little Covid wedding. I would try to explain the feeling of us being called Mama and Mummy, that after all those years of fear I did fall in love and I did make real friends and knowing me, I would probably end up having a little cry for how far we have come.

But then I would have to pull myself together and explain that we are still on the journey. I'd tell her about school gates protests, about shootings in LGBTQIA+ clubs just like the Gates, and about how all over the world, gay people are still living in fear with bigotry against them enshrined in law, facing violence and discrimina-tion. But I'd also tell her about the amazing activists who have worked so hard, and sacrificed so much to make the strides toward equality that we've made. There is more hope than hate but there's still some distance to go.

• • •

I am going to talk to author and activist Ellen Jones about the history of LGBTQIA+ rights, the people across the world still fighting for their love to be recognized and what we can do to help. Once I've triple-checked that I've pressed the record button I begin our chat by asking her if she feels that life has improved for your neighbourhood queer person.

'It depends how far you zoom out in terms of history,' she says. 'Obviously, compared to the time in which it was illegal to be gay in the UK, we've improved significantly and there is some more support in terms of workplaces. There are actual equality protections that exist, but in terms of the day-to-day lived realities, I think we are less secure in the protections that we do have. The UK is slowly sliding down the global rankings in terms of our equality provisions, and we've been condemned by the UN for it.

'I came out when I was fourteen, eleven years ago,' Ellen reveals, 'and I wouldn't come out now today compared to then. It's far too hostile. It feels demonstrably more unsafe. And it's largely to do with the rhetoric that we're seeing, and the sheer escalation of anti-LGBTQIA+ sentiment. You know, when I was at school, I wasn't reading about school children being stabbed to death for being who they were [as happened to trans teenager Brianna Ghey]. That wasn't on my radar, but it's happening now.

'There *are* obviously significant improvements and there's good work being done that wouldn't have previously been possible. But I think we have to be really, really careful about resting on our laurels.

'I think that day to day, there's some safety for some people, but that "some" is doing a lot of hard work because I speak as a cis white lesbian. My experience is very different to that of a working-class Black trans woman in the UK. So the idea of the progress being equal across the community is completely flawed.'

It's sobering to realize that the UK is moving backwards when it comes to equality provisions. With regards to legislation I was interested to know what Ellen feels are the greatest improvements over the last two decades.

'Firstly,' she answers, 'the fact that the Equality Act came into place and that enshrined certain protections into law. There are flaws of the Equality Act in terms of how far it extends and the ways it's being inconsistently applied to trans people, but it's a really key piece of legislation and protection that enables people to start having conversations, start advocating and to start being open and honest about themselves.

'But my key metric is always the conversations I have with folks in the pub. And what I find is that most people are onside with LGBTQIA+ stuff and with queer people more generally. They're quite on board. Even if they don't understand everything, they want people to be able to live their lives. Yes, they have more questions about trans people, and don't always understand that part of the community, but they still, mostly, want them to be able to live freely.'

It's actually interesting that the narratives in the media don't reflect the realities of most people's experience. Ellen continued, 'The British public are broadly accepting of trans people but you wouldn't know that from the press. Most people are pretty chill. And I think compared to twenty years ago, that's not necessarily the attitude that would have been in place. It's partly because of things like Session 28, which wasn't repealed until 2003, and 2006 in Kent. Folk didn't grow up with LGBTQIA+ people around them – as far as they knew. They didn't have that education. Whereas now they have the education, there's more visibility.'

I agreed. So much homophobia and transphobia comes down to an imagined bogeyman. People fear what they don't understand and they don't know. I had only ever really seen Section 28 from my perspective as a queer person but of course it also prevented our straight mates from learning about us and knowing we existed. It prevented straight people from asking questions to help them understand and accept differences.

Ellen is more than ten years younger than me and Section 28 wasn't in place when she was at high school. I wonder if that contributed to her being more of a natural activist than I am.

'With every generation, and rightly so, communities want more acceptance, they want complete equality rather than breadcrumbs that previous generations may have felt were revolutionary.

'One of the things that I always talk about is that the notion of being radical is always contextual. What we might consider here in the UK to be a tokenistic celebration of LGBTQIA+ rights is completely different in another country where people can be killed for being gay. So if a brand or an organization in Ghana, for example, came out with even the smallest line about inclusion, or put a Pride logo on their advert, that would be huge. And I think we have to be mindful of the fact that context is everything and there is no universal solution to getting to where we need to be.'

It's clear to me that we're currently living in a time where it still feels like our rights are sometimes up for debate especially when it comes to trans people within our community. I asked Ellen how I could be a better ally.

'You know,' she tells me, 'I have a certain amount of financial privilege, not everyone has that. So I try and distribute, I pay for people where I can. It's being visible.'

Like going on marches or volunteering?

'Yes, it's about showing up. A lot of activism now happens on social media.'

Do you think it's important to be public in your support online?

'Yes, but one of the things that we can lose sight of, particularly within the online space, which is where a lot of us find community, is nuance. It can be difficult to interpret tone, so a legitimate calling-in can be interpreted as an attack.'

I ask what she means by 'calling-in'.

'I mean acknowledging something that has happened or been said which is not ideal – someone who has misspoken, or spoken out of turn or out of their lane. Calling-in means pointing out when someone has said something ignorant, whether wilfully or not. Because ignorance is always talked about as a pejorative, but actually it's just the state of not knowing something. And there's no way that you can know all human experiences. So it's a way of going, something's happened, you've said something that is harmful, that has implications you probably don't even know.

'It helps to do the education piece and give people the space to retract, to change their minds, to respond. That is a way of showing compassion and an understanding for the nuance. I think we sometimes expect that every queer has gone and done the theory and it creates barriers to community if you're constantly scared that you're not going to say the right thing. Everyone's on a different path. And yeah, you might fuck up, but that's being a human. I don't think 'cancel culture' is a thing particularly, but I do think we can show much more grace and compassion to each other. And we can also just acknowledge that everyone's got different shit going on and we're all trying to survive the best we can.'

I think this is really important. Firstly I agree that cancel culture doesn't really seem to exist. Indeed, when someone is especially transphobic or homophobic in my industry it seems that streamers are lining up to give them millions of dollars. Secondly: Yes, Yes, Yes! (think Meg Ryan) and say it louder for the people in the back. Giving everyone – and I am talking about people within the LGBTQIA+ community *and* our allies – grace and compassion is good for all of us. Now, of course, I am not talking about someone who is preaching hate, spreading lies or profiteering from printing misinformation about marginalized people but if someone's heart is open and they are leading with love, if they get something wrong or misspeak let's correct them but also not berate them for something they just didn't know.

I realize some of you will be reading this, thinking: Suz, I'm reading your book and I am learning loads but I'm

straight, babe, what can I do? Well, I asked Ellen this as well
(you know I've always got your back, babe).

'It starts with listening. It starts with realizing that you
don't know what you don't know. There are different ways
you get your sources. You could go to a leading LGBTQIA+
organization, but again, that's just one perspective. It's good
work to do, but it's just one point of view. I think it's about
getting lots of different perspectives from different sources,
from different LGBTQIA+ people, because we disagree
about things, we're not a monolith.

'I think that's the first thing, and being aware of
the different issues that affect different parts of the
community.

'What can also be really useful is leaning into the issues
in which you already have an interest. So if you care about
climate justice, climate change, go and find out how it's
impacting queer and trans people globally, and find out
who is working in that space who has that identity. If you're
concerned about period poverty, investigate how it dispro-
portionately affects LGBTQIA+ people and why. Make sure
they're a part of your knowledge and your campaigning.

'It can be something that you're already having conversations about. It's about being brave enough to recognize that
you don't know what you don't know, having those conversations, and then doing something afterwards. And that
doing something afterwards could be choosing to donate to
an organization.

'It could be finding out about volunteering opportunities
at your local Pride because they always need people. It could

be writing to your local MP to support a letter or criticize a policy. It's whatever makes sense in your context.'

At the end of the interview, Ellen really gives me something to think about.

'The one final thing that I will say – and sometimes straight and cis people don't realize this – is there's nothing that affects LGBTQIA+ people that *just* affects LGBTQIA+ people. We're seeing this increasingly within trans healthcare, where, in some situations, we have the powers that be deciding that a twenty-five-year-old adult can't make decisions about their own body. That's going to have implications and ramifications across other areas of healthcare.

'If it becomes acceptable for LGBTQIA+ people to be continually homeless, that's going to impact other communities that are affected by homelessness. These things are all interrelated. So on a purely selfish level, you might want to get with the programme. If we're being completely self-serving, even if you hate LGBTQIA+ people, unfortunately, our equality benefits you. So you might want to step that up, unless you are also happy with being treated as lesser.

'Because a system never treats just one group of people as lesser. Just do something.'

Just do something. It's very simple and this isn't me preaching, I am including myself here. If we all engage a little more in being an active ally for marginalized communities it would have an incredible impact.

CHAPTER 10

What is having it all, and do I even want it?

I am tired. Knackered, to be honest. But I want you to know that I *know* I am lucky: lucky to be a mum; lucky to have a job I love and a level of success that means I am writing this book right now. I am also lucky to have my excellent wife. I highly recommend getting one.

If you've read this book in order, you'll know full well that, previous to Alice and Peach, my career took up the greatest chunk of my life. I treated comedy like an Olympic sport and was constantly trying to build my muscle (funnies), condition my body (my persona) and improve my mental stamina and resilience (this one is the same). Resilience has never been my strong suit. I adore stand-up comedy but I have, in my clearer moments, sometimes wondered if a career that is almost completely reliant on validation from strangers is naturally suited to someone as sensitive as me, someone who has struggled with anxiety for her whole life.

This is true of many careers, but in comedy it's particularly hard not to have some sort of jealousy – or at least it

has been for me. Often comedians, especially female comedians, are pitted against each other. There was a time in the
not so distant past when panel shows would have a 'girl'
chair for the one woman that had been booked out of the
six available spots. On one very successful panel show this
was even referred to as the Period Chair by the (all-male)
production team. For a long time, I was obsessed with
getting my turn in that particular chair. I would invite the
booker to shows, write topical jokes for the other comedians
who *were* appearing, and nag Flo to get them to consider me
every series. Eventually I managed to book it, twice, but it
wasn't nearly as fun as I imagined. I spent most of the time
being talked over by a very loud man.

Social media constantly gave me an insight into what
all my contemporaries were doing. Back in the make-up
chair, a comment would read, and my brain would go into
overdrive: What are they recording? Is it a series? Why
haven't I been booked? What have I done wrong? Am I
failing? It's a very self-obsessed attitude, I know. It's kind
of gross but I am being honest. It would always feel like a
personal slight. It's hard for an ardent feminist to accept
those feelings of jealousy towards another woman. Maybe
you've felt something similar at work, in a friendship group,
about a friend's appearance or finances, about a friend
that simply has to look at their partner to end up pregnant
again. It's uncomfortable. I feel uncomfortable admitting
it. And it's hard when it's really in your face, for the whole
world to see. We all know staged shots for social media are
never the real story, only the version of the story someone

is willing to share, but even though I know that, I have still found it painful to witness. And comedy and TV work can sometimes feel like social media on steroids. For example, if I went up for a job as an account manager at a graphic design company, prepared really hard, smashed the interview but didn't get the role, it would of course be gutting. I'd guess it would take me a few weeks, maybe a couple of months, to get over it. But if I get close but miss out on a telly or comedy job not only do I know exactly who was chosen over me, and get to obsess over all the possible reasons why, but I have to see my failure advertised on TV and emblazoned on billboards. I have to see glossy weekend supplements hailing the comic who did get the role as the Future of Funny and witness all the subsequent jobs that they land as a result. But I must be clear, this competitiveness was never about not wanting other women to win. I always want women to win but there was a period where I felt that someone else's win confirmed my place as a loser, somewhere I remembered viscerally from the long lunch breaks walking the school corridors alone.

The homophobia I've encountered from people in the industry, sometimes subtle – 'Could you wear something other than a suit, you've got a good figure, what about a dress?' – occasionally blatant, was the salt in the wound. Once, at a birthday party of a very successful comedian, a drunk TV producer told me: 'The trouble with you is, you're very funny but no one knows where to put a lesbian. Audiences are just a lot more comfortable with gay men, and we already have Sue Perkins.' Wow. TV already had one acceptable lesbian so how could there possibly be room for me? That particular encounter woke up the latent homophobia that lives inside me. I started to worry that I would be making audiences uncomfortable by virtue of just being me, that something in me that I couldn't change was inherently unlikeable. Sometimes, I would envy other female comedians not so much for the opportunities they got, but because who they went to bed or fell in love with wasn't a hindrance to their career.

But having a life outside of my career has helped me see the bigger picture. I realized I didn't want to spend my whole life feeling little stabs of envy when a colleague got their own TV show or a sitcom commissioned. The idea of that going on for ever exhausted me, but it wasn't just that. It made me judge myself. I didn't want to be that guy. I'd had a taste of it, and now I wanted to create a whole life, one that included love, family, friendship *and* work, but where I was too fulfilled to worry about what someone else was doing.

Many of the achievements I've made in my career have been down to hard work. I think I have some talent. I am not the most gifted comedian of my generation – heck, I am not the most gifted comedian in my close friendship group – but I work hard and I write a lot. Some of my opportunities have come from this dedication, work ethic and talent. But some of them are just luck. I have been at the right place at the right time. In 2017 someone saw me doing studio warm-up for a sitcom, a truly thankless task where you're the filler no one has asked for while actors change costumes and cameras move around the studio. I was warming up on a big BBC One sitcom, when there was some sort of issue with lighting and I had to do more than thirty minutes of stand-up. The audience was up for it and I had a lovely gig. It was lucky I had been on tour opening for Josh Widdicombe the week before so I felt match fit. It was lucky that there was a problem with the lighting. It just so happened a bigwig from the Beeb was at the record. *That* was lucky too. He liked my material and I ended up landing a thirty-minute spot on *Live from the BBC*, which was my first ever proper telly job. That record went really well (probably down to some talent and a lot of hard work travelling around the country honing the material) and less than a year later I was doing panel shows and appearing on *Live at the Apollo*.

So some of it's down to talent, some down to hard work and some because of luck.

But luck can be a fickle thing and, I finally began to see, if all my self-worth was wrapped up in work success and so much of my work success was reliant on luck, I was going to be in tricky territory.

There's nothing like the twin earthquakes of a global pandemic and becoming a parent to give you a dose of realism when it comes to how important being funny for money is. The combination of Peach and very few gigs gave me permission to stop, something I had never really done before. I'd worked right from when I was a teenager. I had weekend jobs and summer jobs throughout my education and training, then I had the wild juggle of odd jobs and stand-up gigs when I was trying to make a go of it as a comedian. And I liked it: a full diary keeps my brain in check, being busy keeps the worries at bay. I've never had much spare time and I've never wanted it. On some level, I think I was frightened of what would happen if I did ever have to stop, but in 2020 it was taken out of my hands. I had an abundance of spare time. Before Peach came home Alice and I had never spent so many hours together. We cooked together, played board games, built Lego, watched box sets. I read all the books I had always planned to read and it was joyful. We had the time and space to begin the adoption journey. I finally allowed myself to stop. The world had given me permission to focus on my family and on myself. And, to my surprise, it felt amazing. But I knew it couldn't last for ever.

By autumn 2021, work had really picked up. Live gigs were open again, my latest tour's twenty-month hiatus had ended, stand-up was back and it felt great. I'd really missed making people laugh. The electricity of a live show. The buzz. As usual, I took every gig I could. I quickly slipped back into pre-Covid Suz and got to work: pedal to the metal. Alongside trying to be a present and good mum, I was driving around the country for gigs, hosting three podcasts, filming bits for telly, pitching shows and trying to write scripts. The juggle was real but I am a comedian, you have to be a polymath, that's the job. And that level of physical and mental intensity meant my anxiety didn't make a peep until bedtime. But, of course, it was still there. As I snuggled into bed all the thoughts would come: the mum guilt, the fear that I was putting too much pressure on Alice, anxieties about imagined scenarios, financial concerns about the future. I once woke up at 3 a.m. and loudly announced: 'But I don't have a pension.' The worry tank was filling up but I convinced myself that – as ever – more work would fix it. I was constantly telling myself: 'I just need to get to next week then it'll all calm down a bit.' It never calmed down.

In July 2022, I was booked for the Montreal Comedy Festival. The biggest comedy showcase across the pond. That festival felt like a big deal. With Edinburgh anyone can book a room and put on a show but to go to Montreal you had to be invited. I had been banging on the bookers' door for six or seven years, so I was delighted to be finally flown to Canada to try my hand in front of a North American crowd as part of a showcase for new international talent. I got on the plane with pain in my lower back. A few weeks before, I had been driving through Morocco with the brilliant Maisie Adam for a TV show called *World's Most Dangerous Roads*. Six days driving a massive jeep alongside a cliff edge had taken its toll. It had left me achy at best and in agony at worst. The day I returned from Morocco I visited the osteopath; I had done some damage to a disc and irritated a facet joint (don't recommend, one star). The osteo asked if I had been under a lot of pressure, and how was my mental health? Was this a physical manifestation of something else? I shrugged it off. It irritated me that this osteopath had made assumptions about my mental well-being. She didn't know me. Didn't she realize I was just trying to get shit done? I was striving for a career that wouldn't only support my family, but would also be creatively fulfilling and have longevity. I decided she was probably lazy. She likely only worked Monday to Friday and used her evenings and weekends for fun and life-affirming time with friends and family – what a dweeb.

Despite quite acute pain, I decided I couldn't pass up an opportunity to perform in Montreal. I know we were in Canada, but the festival would be full of the biggest American talent agents and casting scouts, I could get snapped up: this time next year I could be a movie star, my Del Boy dad's optimism rang in my ears as I packed my bag and left for the airport. I was so lucky that Tom Allen was also at the festival. I knew I had a partner in crime for dinner and wine and a real friend if the festival got overwhelming. I arrived feeling pretty good, I had been given some painkillers and sedatives for the flight and boy, did they work. The first night, I did a couple of gigs in small rooms to warm up my set for the two showcases. They were fun. It seemed my short set travelled well. I was so used to being onstage for more than an hour on tour it felt I was on and off again in a flash. It was a bit odd to be flown all that way to do two seven-minute sets, in the hope that the American industry will see you and sign you up, allowing you to apply for an American visa and potentially work in the States. Side stage at the first gig, I was on last and I felt confident. The compère, my friend Ed Gamble, said my name and on I went. I had a great gig. Big laughs. I felt relaxed and playful. I came offstage, satisfied. Then, the pain in my back struck like a lightning bolt. I hurried into a dressing room and shut the door. I was embarrassed. I got on all fours and rocked back and forth just like the osteo had shown me. Something released, and thank goodness, I was OK, for now. I gathered myself and went to join the other stand-ups and Lily (a brilliant agent from Off the Kerb, who had come with us). I feared admitting the back pain would somehow reveal a weakness. I wanted to appear strong, I don't know why. Lily hugged me and confirmed I'd had a great gig. On the way out of the theatre I was stopped by a big American agent. He told me he loved my stuff, and asked if I was interested in a career in America? He was going to come to the second showcase and bring some of the team. I was well aware, though, that, in my experience, this is how American agents talk – you can't trust them. You never have a bad meeting with an American in my industry. Like professional pick-up artists, they'll promise you the world, then leave you high and dry – but still it felt exciting, and surely for every twenty comedians they meet, there must be one that makes it Stateside. Maybe this time, that one would be me. I played it cool – 'Great, let's chat' – but inside I was already tearfully holding an Emmy and thanking my mum.

I was in pain the entire trip but I just ignored it. Nothing bad ever happens from ignoring emotional and physical pain, right? I was also really homesick and FaceTiming Alice and Peach whenever I could. The following day, I headed down to showcase number 2. The American agents had confirmed their attendance. Backstage, suited and booted, hair quiffed, red lippy on, I was ready. The lights went down in the auditorium. Then all of a sudden, a drill, there was a fire alarm. We all ignored it. Because it was clearly a false alarm. Then a very stressed teenager came to usher us outside to the safety point. Eurgh, this means the show will start at least twenty minutes late, we all thought, and then we saw actual smoke billowing under a door. Fuck. Then water pouring down the fire exit stairs. Shit. We waited outside for ten, twenty, thirty minutes. The four-hundred-strong audience dissipated. I watched the American agent and his team stroll away, heads in a programme, deciding whose show they'd drop in on instead, taking my imaginary Emmy with them. The show was cancelled and we all trundled to a bar, unsure of what else to do. That night there was a big party hosted by Netflix. Everyone performing at the festival had been invited. Everyone was very excited to go, and we were told it would be an amazing opportunity to network. Americans love to network. It doesn't really make sense to me. Surely, you'll book a job on the strength of your material rather than by having some chitchat at a party with a glass of room-temperature wine. Also, I am not a natural at chitchat. I once panicked after being introduced to Clare Balding and said: 'So you love horses?' She just smiled.

Tom felt similarly about the party and Lily agreed, so instead of a glamorous Netflix party we found a French bistro and drank some really nice Sancerre. I got home a little bit pissed and decided to have a shower. Being a bit merry I must have been generous with the shower gel because I slipped and stumbled, twisted and somehow ended up on the floor – imagine Bambi learning to walk or a toddler trying roller skates for the first time. Bollocks. I was in agony. I burst into tears, then crawled out of the shower and wrapped myself in a towel. The shock had knocked me sober. And now I couldn't stop crying. I struggled to the bed and laid in the foetal position and sobbed. The back pain was part of it but I had opened the floodgates. The worry tank had built to a point where the dam could no longer hold it back.

I missed Alice. I missed Peach. I felt really very lonely. What was I doing in Canada, trying to impress these people, when my girls were so far away? I looked through the pictures Alice had sent me throughout the day, them at the park, Peach at Rhyme Time clapping along, her dancing in the kitchen saying: 'Mama Mama.' A ten-minute walk from my hotel room was a party with some of the global movers and shakers in comedy but I didn't care. I was just desperate to be at home, dancing in the kitchen. I didn't want to miss a trip to the park or Rhyme Time. I didn't want Peach asking for 'Mama' and wondering where I was. Whilst I still loved stand-up, I realized at that moment that I didn't *need* it in the way I once had. The addition of Alice and Peach, the love I felt at home meant I wasn't compelled to go searching for validation in quite the same way. I needed to get some balance. In that hotel room, weeping in a towel, something in my mind clicked. A switch wasn't completely turned off but the dimmer twisted, and the fluorescent light mellowed. For the first time in more than a decade, being a stand-up needed to stop being my first descriptor. It had always been my identity but now it wasn't and that felt good.

I did fear that my appetite for the hustle would have a detrimental effect on my career. I had grafted for so long to start making a good living from comedy, to create a touring audience and be someone who occasionally popped up on telly, and whilst I had achieved a lot on my career dream list, there was more I wanted to do. But something changed. It seemed that the imaginary clock that had always ticked so loudly behind me went quiet. I no longer felt like I was in a race. The competitive side of me seemed to fade away. I realized a career was long but Peach would only be a little Peach for a few short years. So, whilst I didn't entirely take my foot off the gas – I was still working five days a week – I moved into third gear and prioritized playdates and bedtimes for the time being. I'm aware, again, how lucky I am to be in a position where I was able to make the choice to do that.

I've had countless chats with women working in various sectors about when 'the right' time to have a baby is. Not directly after starting a new job, not too young but equally not too old, not when there's a busy year at work ahead, not at a time when you could be seen as replaceable. But I don't think there's ever a right time and sometimes when people feel they've reached the 'right' time the baby doesn't happen. What I am trying to say is, I decided to focus on what I had, rather than reaching for something that might never be.

I had to decide what success looked like all over again. What did it look like now, with a family? With my mental and physical well-being taken into consideration? How did I really want my life to be set up? I knew loads of performers who had put the job first, spent years on the road chasing the bright lights, always needing that next hit of a bigger audience, more money, more fame. They didn't all seem happy. Fame is a strange thing. Mine is at the low level which means sometimes on the train people stare at me wondering whether I am a bit famous or was I in the year below them at school. Frequently, I get confused for some other stand-up comedian. Once, a drunk woman told me she loved my routine about my twins. I explained that's not me, that's Jen Brister. This woman wouldn't have it. She argued with me, trying to convince me that I did, in fact, have twins. She was such an adept debater she made me question myself. When I got home I double-checked there was only one child in Peach's bedroom.

It's true that, for a while, I really wanted to be very famous. Like Taylor Swift famous. I am quite embarrassed to admit it (Christ, I am constantly telling you everything; writing a book is extremely exposing) and whilst it's not unusual to want to be a celebrity, I do now think it is quite cringe. I thought being famous looked awesome but I don't think it's what I thought it was when I was a teenager, searching to belong. I thought it meant a very easy life, where you have loads of friends and a pool, but actually it seems quite demanding and tiresome; also I think having a pool is actually a bit of a faff. I have friends that are famous, very famous, ripple of excitement when they enter a restaurant famous, and it looks exhausting. They have the fame, they have countless options when it comes to work and fun opportunities. They have lots of money and awards and things that make you feel special, but they also have the pressure, the tabloids, the people stopping them for a selfie when they're trying to have dinner with their kids, and the fear that it might all go away.

I needed to work out what I wanted and not only that, I had to work out what I could cope with. I have been known to get so overwhelmed I become useless, frozen to the spot, sometimes to a bed in a Canadian hotel. And when I only had myself to worry about that wasn't a huge issue. I could book a massage or run to a gym class or go out for some wine with a pal but now I had Peach, now she relied on me I had to find a way to keep the anxiety at a distance, to keep the pressure on but at a low heat, at a temperature I could maintain. After years of worshipping the hustle it had become unsustainable. I know that we celebrate being a girl boss. But I had come to the realization that I am not, and also don't want to be, a girl boss. I will be a girl junior manager on my very best day. I once read a day plan of someone who described themselves as a She E O (like CEO but pink). To factor in exercise she had to get up at 4.30 a.m. because her day was so packed. She had a smoothie for lunch so she could 'load up' on the move and would do emails in bed before she slept. This woman had millions, a massive company, a gorgeous house but f**k me, that sounds like hell. When did she enjoy the fruits of her labour? She had a wine cellar but I doubt she ever had time to invite some mates round for a bottle of the really really good Pinot. She had the perfect party house, a sound system that could rival any nightclub, more room to dance than the *Strictly* ballroom set but it always looked pristine and clean and I doubted very much that anyone had ever slut-dropped on her kitchen block. What a shame.

I do still work hard. I still tour the country, write stand-up shows, do podcasts, and have written a book, but when I get home I turn off. And you know the incredible thing? It's actually made me better at my job. Having a life outside of comedy has not only made me happier but it has made me better at comedy. I would sooner have less money and more of Peach and Alice and feel like the work I am creating has value. I know I am lucky that I get to choose to have more work-life balance, that I have a level of security that I can say no to jobs that don't work for the three of us. I am truly lucky and grateful that I have a choice as I know that the majority of people don't. But I still don't think it's possible to have it all and now I know I don't want it.

. . .

I am going to talk to my friend, fellow comedian and mother Sara Pascoe. I met Sara when I first started on the stand-up circuit and have always looked up to her. I want to know how she's faced these challenge and what advice she might have for the rest of us.

I ask her how becoming a mum changed her relationship to her career.

'At the beginning of parenthood I was working a diary that I'd made before and during pregnancy. *You* know, we put our work in six months, a year, eighteen months in advance. I was working out a diary that was very hard, because I had no idea what it was going to be like to have a child.

'So I was contractually obliged to film a documentary when I had a four-month-old, and it was so hard for me and my family. The restrictions of filming – they wouldn't let the baby visit me on set and I couldn't store pumped milk – meant I had to stop breastfeeding. I also didn't get to see him for twelve hours a day, at a stage where I was so hormonal and attached to him. And I tried to underplay how hard I found it in case they thought I was being a drama queen.'

I am so shocked by this. It's obviously totally unacceptable but also a real indication of how little experience massive channels have with working mothers.

'It was really difficult,' Sara agrees. 'And I didn't know how to advocate myself because I'd never been a mum before, and everything had been agreed while I was pregnant. The job had been moved because of Covid and I'd agreed to that, so it was really, really tough. I was all just like, "OK, just get through it", basically because I didn't want to essentially fall out with the channel because they are a pretty big employer.'

That must have been awful. I can't imagine the stress.

'I don't remember doing that filming,' Sara says. 'That's how stressed I was. I just had to get through it.'

She goes on to confirm how far from unusual that situation was.

'On series we often film thirteen-hour days. TV's not made around parents balancing looking after small kids. If you look at how many women in our age group are having children, that is what people are juggling.

'There's never rest time built into it. It's only work and children, no social life. So that was how it was for me at the very beginning and then I did learn a little bit in terms of not doing the same when I had the second one.

'Because what I didn't understand is the level to which children affect your life. You don't – you can't – put kids away. They're not like older kids, they don't go to school, there is no time. They're your responsibility all of the time. And when I say it's a struggle, it's not like I'm miserable, but I lost a part of my life that had previously obsessed me, fascinated me. I was so passionate about my work and I'm not able to be there any more. It's the equivalent of . . . you know how you used to eat meals before you had a young child? You sat down at a plate, and it was all yours, and you got to finish it.

'And then when you have a young child, you sort of grab things that have fallen on the floor from them, things they haven't finished. I mean, why bother making myself food when you're not going to eat those fish fingers? And you sort of think: am I the bin? Am I the bin? Just sort of tidying up with my mouth?

'That's how I feel about my career now. It's like, I'm really happy if I can just grab a moment.'

Despite the challenges, I tell Sara that I felt being a mother has made me better at stand-up. Sara agrees.

'First of all, I thought it made me worse, and that's because I was so worried all the time about the child. You're out at work, but you're very conscious of other things. Are they asleep? Is my partner OK? Will the trains be delayed on the way home?

'It's all stuff I used to not worry about. I just could concentrate on the gig, focus on it, and get it. Also, I was obsessed with stand-up, so I thought about my material all the time. When I had my first son, I couldn't do that. You know, I'd just arrive at the venue and go straight on, I didn't get a chance to do any showbiz click, any, like, energy of: Hey, I'm here!

'I felt so raw and it felt shit for a number of months. And then I realized that because I was finally, finally myself on stage, everything suddenly became better.

'But since the material started to fit it, I now think I'm so much more connected to what I'm saying all the time. It's what I was trying to do before, which is not fake anything, actually be there in the moment. So my off-the-cuff stuff is better. And I'm not having these massive crashes afterwards. I used to come offstage and feel like ugh, like depression within fifteen minutes. I don't have it any more, I'm just a person on the way home now. You know, it feels like a job.'

I ask Sara whether that's changed what success looks like for her now.

'Success only matters if someone's happy. It's really easy to have all the stuff and be miserable. And then thus undermining the whole fucking point.

'And so that's where I think things like therapy or self-help books or just doing the work alongside it are so important. We live in the best country in the world, and I don't mean that in a "Rule Britannia" way, I mean in terms of how lucky we are to live here, with where we are in terms of having rights and money and choices.

'It's important that you have something that you like to do with your off time, when you have a moment and you are just contented like a fat cat. That's what we should feel like, shouldn't we? Like fun for the day. Reading my book in the bath. That's what I think success looks like, being able to enjoy the off time.

'Because you're not in a race with yourself any more, and

you're not in a panic about what everyone else in the world is doing. And you can appreciate that now. I think contentedness is probably the word. But that doesn't mean that you don't have ambition or ideas. It just means that you're actually also enjoying the process.'

I am getting so much better at appreciating this bit now but it is always useful to be reminded. When I interviewed Elizabeth Day in Chapter 4, we discussed professional jealousy and her words and advice were far too good to leave out. They fit perfectly as a little bonus to this chapter. I asked Elizabeth whether she thought that professional jealousy was inevitable.

'I guess there might be a few discrete individuals,' she says, 'who believe so fundamentally in the purpose of what they're doing work-wise that it's, in and of itself, its own motivation. They understand that they have their own lane and their own universe that they are the centre of, and they are not inspired or motivated by anyone else's path. Now, I can only aspire to be that enlightened. That has not been my experience. I think that's like one of the goals of a meaningful life, but I'm going to spend my life trying to get there. For most of us, professional jealousy is another thing that we can repackage in the same way that we can repackage disappointment.

'Because very often I'm jealous because someone is doing something that I would like to be doing, or they're achieving something at a level that I would like to be achieving at. And therefore, is there a way of looking at that and saying: OK, what is it that that represents for me? What is it that triggers this feeling of jealousy?

'Because the jealousy probably comes from something in your past like Jillian taking your best friend Karen away from you at primary school, and it probably isn't necessarily wholly attached to the professional thing that you're experiencing. So could you try and dismantle it a bit and think: OK, well, what does that person have? Or what do they represent that I would like in myself? And how can I go about trying to get that for myself? And then you can make the motivation more positive.'

Elizabeth pauses for a moment. 'Wait,' she says. 'Am I talking about jealousy, or envy? What's the difference?'

We break off our chat to have a quick check of dictionary.com. It tells us that envy can be described as a mix of admiration and discontent, but it's not necessarily malicious whereas jealousy is a feeling of resentment, bitterness, or hostility toward someone who has something that you don't. It's clear to me that what both Elizabeth and I experience is envy – a longing and wanting for something, but no malice involved.

'The problem with envy, if it's left unchecked, is that you turn it inwards. You think: well, I'm terrible and I'm failing and I'm rubbish and I'm a negative pile of excrement. And that's not a healthy space to approach professional fulfilment from. It's far healthier to think: OK, so this person has shown me a way forward, and something I could do slightly differently, so why don't I try that?'

Sage words, Day, sage indeed.

Epilogue

Writing this book has been a hugely cathartic experience. I came across memories I didn't know I still had, covered in dust but still recognizable. Writing them down has encouraged me to be more honest than I had planned to be.

But when I have been in an anxious pit, what I have searched for is truth – truthfulness about what it feels like to have a brain like mine. So here's my truth. Maybe it will be of help to someone. I always assumed I was special, that my brain was unique or at the very least interesting, but in talking to ten brilliant people about the mucky ins and outs of being alive, I've realized my brain, my heartache, my failure, my anxiety are all pretty normal. That they're pretty commonplace. That I am not that special after all. The realization of that normality has helped with the shame. I have stopped trying to fix it. I have stopped trying to win. I have accepted anxiety as my friend for life, have accepted that sometimes she's helped me, that she's kept me safe or made me work hard, or given me the focus and obsession to create something to be proud of. And at other times she's really fucked things up and stolen my sleep.

But either way she is mine and accepting her has eased my busy brain. Maybe this book will help you accept yours. I hope so. It won't be a permanent fix though. She'll still pop in unannounced and stay for longer than you'd like, but on those nights when it all feels a bit much, I breathe or dance or talk to the moon (or even my nan) and trust the tide will turn.

I have learnt a lot about what it means to live and take chances, to really go for gold. To accept your failures and your shortcomings, and to admit when you're wrong, especially to a child. I really hope this book gives you the push you need to go for that job, or mend your broken heart, to be your authentic self, to find love, to commit to your life and simply take your worries along for the ride.

I'm having more fun now. I hope you are too.

Acknowledgements

The first person I need to thank is my editor Jodie, it's been a joy to work with you and your encouragement, support and notes made this book so much better. Thanks for listening to all my worries (although you commissioned a book about anxiety, so you have no one to blame but yourself). Big thanks also to the whole team at Bluebird/ Pan Macmillan, I have loved this experience.

Flo, my manager and my friend. You changed my life. Thank you for not letting me quit stand up, for always giving great advice and for helping me get that work–life balance. #TheJuggle.

Thank you to the whole team at Off The Kerb for always looking after me, especially in the early days when you regularly gave me an advance to cover my rent. Big shout out to Lily, Katy Helps, Katy A, Antonia, Kizzi, Ann and Hayley.

Thanks to my friends for their love and support in no particular order, Tom, Jenny, Ruth, Ross, Laura, Clare, Gaby,

Josh, Romesh, Maisie, Rosie, Amanda, Trak, Diana and Faye and also Faye's mum and dad, Lesley and Clyde who had me as a house guest for far too long when I first pursued stand-up.

Such huge thanks to the experts I spoke to for the book, your time and insights helped it become what I dreamt it might be: Dr Kirren Schnack, Natasha Devon, Owen O'Kane, Elizabeth Day, Dolly Alderton, Charlene Douglas, Laura Bates, Ellen Jones, Dr Martha Deiros Collado and Sara Pascoe.

Thanks to Dawn French for some great advice.

Thank you to my family, my cousins Hollie, Sophie, Natalie and Jodie for always supporting what I'm doing and always checking in and all my aunties and uncles.

My mother-in-law Gill, thanks for all the support and advice.

Mum, thank you for always believing in me and for the hours spent driving to classes and clubs when I was a teen. Dad, thanks for always answering the phone at midnight when I am driving home and need a bit of company. Joe, a great brother and a great friend.

Alice, you get the gist how much I love you from the chapter about us. Thank you for letting me share part of our life and for your constant support.

Peach, being your Mama is the greatest part of my life.

And finally, to you, thank you for reading this book, thanks for coming on this journey, writing it was liberating but really bloody exposing too. I hope it's helped you in some small way, given you hope and made you laugh.